Prepping for
SUCCESS

The Ultimate Handbook
For The Beginner
HIGH SCHOOL BASKETBALL COACH

Michael J. Coffino

Prepping for Success: The Ultimate Handbook For
The Beginner High School Basketball Coach
© 2019, Michael J. Coffino. All Rights Reserved.
Published by A&I Publishing, Tiburon, California

978-1-7336688-0-4 (paperback)
978-1-7336688-1-1 (ebook)

Prepping for **SUCCESS**

Also by Michael J. Coffino

*My Life: A Story of Resilience and Love
(Summer of 2019)*

*The Other Classroom: The Essential
Importance of High School Athletics*

*Odds-On Basketball Coaching: Crafting High-
Percentage Strategies for Game Situations*

*Play It Forward: From Gymboree
to the Yoga Mat and Beyond*

Dedication

I dedicate this book to a lineage of coaches who have inspired and influenced me over five decades, foremost, my enormously talented brother Coach John Coffino and my first coaching mentor Coach Eliot Smith (Lick-Wilmerding High School), as well as late coaches Dan Buckley (La Salle Academy), Jerome Domershick (CCNY), and—not the least—John Wooden (UCLA). Thank you for teaching me that an essential part of our work as coaches is what we pass on to other coaches.

Contents

Preface

Several years ago, when one of my sons got his first high school coaching job as the head coach of a high school frosh-soph basketball team, I offered to put thoughts on paper to prepare him for the exciting opportunity. I had been a varsity basketball head coach at different schools for quite awhile at the time. Each coaching gig presented different challenges and opportunities, and I knew well the breadth of responsibility awaiting him, even with a lower level team.

I began with a checklist. But as I probed my own experiences, the checklist morphed into a comprehensive outline of the tasks and challenges high school head coaches have to handle. After giving him the finished product and wishing him luck, I left him to study its contents. He has thrived as a high school and youth club coach.

When I later mentioned that fatherly exercise to fellow high school varsity head coaches, they encouraged me to build out and publish the work to allow other young coaches to benefit from what it had to offer. I liked the idea and the finished product follows. In addition to my twenty-four years of coaching experience, the book draws on contributions from referees, athletic directors, the media, and coaches who were kind enough to provide their perspectives. My hope is that this book will help aspiring and beginner high school varsity head basketball coaches, as well as beginners as other levels, build strong and resilient basketball programs and improve the quality of the high school basketball experience for student-athletes, schools, and communities.

Introduction

Many in the public arena perceive the high school basketball coach in a singular role, an eager adult pacing feverishly in front of a bench in a noisy gym for thirty-two minutes of action, directing and exhorting athletes to the pursuit of victory. Others might cast them as glorified physical education teachers. Both are light years from reality.

Often unappreciated are the countless hours and days coaches devote discharging an array of responsibilities beyond what occurs during a game or the quieter confines of a practice facility. High school varsity basketball head coaches wear multiple hats: administrator, coach, teacher, manager, leader, communicator and relationship-builder, community organizer, fundraiser, role model, public relations promoter, and mentor. Each commands specific skills and each has its own learning curve. Together they comprise a collection of tasks both fascinating and dizzying.

As role models, varsity head coaches are called upon to teach myriad life lessons to their student-athletes. They must be trust-building listeners and develop keen communication skills to build relationships with an array of people, including school administrative personnel and teachers, their athletic director, a diverse corps of game referees, other coaches, and community members. They must learn how to navigate often delicate situations with parents and forge understandings and expectations with them to produce consistently positive impacts on players. They need a vision, foreseeing how to build a thriving basketball program based on core values. Each year they must assume the role of master planner and scheduler as they work with countless coaches, parents, and others to organize virtually an entire year full of multiple activities. They often are compelled to work closely with school systems that monitor academic performance so athletes can handle their student-athlete responsibilities and receive proper support when necessary. Every now and then, they must transform into salesperson and marketer to create a buzz in the local community about the basketball program and incite a procession of fans into the gym for home games. They must become media savvy so they can draw maximum positive attention to the program. They must learn to understand, cope with, and embrace the challenges teenagers face *outside* the gym that impact how they perform *in* the gym. And, oh yes, they have to teach the game of basketball and manage game competition. That multi-faceted job description is not for the faint of heart. "Labor of love" is custom-made for what high school coaches do. Coaches coach because they have a heartfelt passion for the game and a powerful desire to teach values and impart lessons that will keep high school athletes in good stead well beyond their athletic careers. But passion and desire will only take you so far. You also need know-how.

This book is a comprehensive source of help. It tracks and explores the seemingly countless things beginner varsity head basketball coaches must learn to build an effective and value-based program. The complexity of the job means it cannot and should not be done alone. Guidance and support systems are key. This book, therefore, is not for the coach who wants to wing it. It is designed for the coach who wants to do the best job of which they are capable and build the best program they can build at the high school where they find themselves.

You as coaches will face limitations in the form of rules, policies, and the working styles of others. Know, however, that restrictions do not mean you cannot find consistent expression for your passion and mission within the borders of your situation. Be doggedly creative and pursue your vision with conviction.

One cautionary note: not every detail or nuance in this book will apply to your situation. Schools, cultures, personnel, and rules can differ greatly from school to school, region to region, and state to state. This book is comprehensive in the sense it covers what I believe aspiring and beginner head basketball coaches in high school need to know and think about to build a thriving basketball program. Your situation will require different considerations here and there, and you can adapt accordingly. The process of change is never-ending.

The best coaches never stop learning and are unafraid to make mistakes—and be assured you will make your fair share of them. Treat each error as a stepping stone for growth and greater knowledge. Be incessantly hungry for information to help you be a more effective coach, whether derived from clinics, books, online videos, DVDs, or the insights of others. Have your own style and find your true coaching voice. Be willing to change as you learn.

I hope this book serves a valuable resource to guide you in your early years as a basketball head coach and helps you build dynamic programs on your terms.

Getting a High School
Head Coaching Job

Potential head coaching positions in high school sprout in various ways (e.g., from an existing position at the school, word of mouth, and as advertised on websites or other listings). Pursue each coveted job opening thoughtfully, diligently, and with enthusiasm. Here are suggestions for navigating the process.

1. *Personal References.* Whether requested or not, assemble two or three references (or whatever is required). If possible, each reference should represent different vantage points (e.g., a coach, an employer, former teacher or school advisor, an athletic director, community representative, and so on). The references should focus at least in part on the natural fit between you and the school and position. For example, if the program

is rebuilding, the references should stress your patience and long-term vision capability, among other traits and selling points. Know what the school wants.

2. *Cover Letter and Resume.* Appearances are important in any materials you supply to a school. Content is key of course, but how you present yourself in writing is as important as how you dress for an interview. Be proud of how your resume looks. Proofread carefully!

The internet teems with pointers and advice about how to write cover letters and resumes. Here are personal preferences:

- Don't simply dust off and update an existing resume. Tailor the resume to the job. Present your experiences in a manner that speaks to the coaching opportunity. This does not mean leaving other stuff out, only what to feature.

- Be factually accurate and don't overstate. Keep in mind that if you leave chronological gaps, you likely will be asked about them in interviews.

- Include any awards that speak to your character.

- The cover letter, while not being dramatic, should begin with an attention-grabbing sentence or two. Incite the reader to read more.

- Limit the cover letter to one page, using crisp and relatively short sentences. Don't regurgitate resume content. Expand why you are well suited for the position. Be personal and speak to the basketball program you want to steward.

3. *Diligence on the School Culture.* Get reasonably familiar with the school, its culture, and the athletic program. Understand institutional values, priorities, and goals. While sometimes difficult, canvas as many people as practical who will speak candidly about the school. This will aid you immeasurably in interviews and making a decision, if you get the offer.

4. *Confer with Other Coaches.* If practical and appropriate, confer with the prior head coach as well as current coaches at the school. While you might have to discount some of what they say, they might preview what life will be like day to day if you get the job.

5. *The Coach-School "Fit."* Coaches sometimes pursue head positions without regard for whether their style, philosophy, and values mesh with school culture. They just want the job. Assessing "fit," however, which requires self-awareness and self-honesty, can be enlightening. For example, will you be able to communicate effectively—meaning, will you be heard—in the particular school culture. Do your values resonate with those of the school? How will your coaching style harmonize with how the athletic director (AD) likes to run the athletic ship?

Diligence notwithstanding, you likely will not get a complete picture of whether the fit is right and, to some extent, will have to trust your instincts. The fit is not always there and jumping into a situation where you sense incompatibility can be risky, in both the short and long term. Courage and long-term vision might mean you pass up something available in favor of waiting for the right opportunity.

6. *Performance History and Other Relevant Facts.* Every program has a track record—good or bad, up or down, consistent or inconsistent. Understand where the program has been and is likely to go. Be prepared to discuss where you will take the program—and how.

7. *Interviews.* No matter how strong your resume and references, the interview process is what will put you over the top. Coaching position interviews can take various forms and multiple stages, including phased individual and group sessions with the AD, select players, school administrators, teachers, and sometimes parents.

Preparation is essential. Be prepared to demonstrate keen knowledge of the school and its athletic program and focus on how, in that environment, you will lead the program, not how the position is good for you and your career. Consider bringing materials that show your approach to the game, like statements of your coaching philosophy, writings, and sample practice sheets. Be direct and responsive in your answers and do not ramble. Be confident but not cocky. Avoid negativity, especially about the former coach. Look professional!

Be especially sensitive to how you interact with ADs during interviews. In relative terms, most ADs are more interested in personality fit than how much you know about basketball. They know that, unlike personality, knowledge can be acquired and ADs place great value on harmonious and mutually beneficial relationships with their coaches. Some personalities succeed at some schools and not others, no matter how encyclopedic the basketball mind.

Sell your positive attributes. Be open about who you are and how you work. Share your working style and ask about the AD's working style, vision, and expectations. Together, explore the fit. This sort of openness shows you have given significant thought to what is important to succeed as a head coach at that school and have the grounding necessary to fill the roles expected of you.

Come armed with questions that both are important to you and demonstrate preparation and readiness. And, of course, be prepared to address a wide array of subjects you may be asked about. They can include, among other things:

• A brief statement of yourself.

- Your coaching philosophy (for thoughts, see Chapter 2 on Building a Program and Chapters 16 and 17 on Defense and Offense, respectively).
- Your vision for the program.
- How you approach the coach mentoring role.
- How you would handle behavioral problems (e.g., off-campus drinking or drug use, an irate parent, unsportsmanlike conduct in games, or academic problems).
- The qualities a good coach possesses (and which of them you possess).
- Your coaching strengths and weaknesses (or needed areas of growth).
- How you define a successful basketball program.
- The comparative importance to you between winning and producing a fun athletic environment.
- What singular quality you want the community to identify with your program.
- What values you would seek to advance.
- Your long-term coaching goals and aspirations.
- Whether you would treat every player the same and if not, why not.
- Why you want to coach at this school.
- Your philosophy on discipline.
- What your typical practice is like.
- How you would handle tryout cuts.
- The qualities you favor in assistant coaches.

- How you would communicate plans and expectations to parents.
- How you see the proper role of parents in the basketball program.
- How you would address playing time concerns of players.
- How you would handle player commitments to other activities that might interfere with how you want to run the program.
- Your personal coaching role models—and why them.
- What you have learned from prior coaching experiences.
- Your best and worst coaching memories.
- Finally, if you really want to kick it up a notch, consider having someone mock interview you. A practice run or two will help steel you for the real thing, in the same way practices do for games.

8. *Follow Up.* After the formal process is over and you await a decision, promptly send a note—an email is fine—to express thanks to everyone you met for their time and your continued enthusiasm for the job.

Once you get the job, get right to work.

Building a Basketball Program and Culture

A high school head coaching position is a special opportunity. It is a chance to create a basketball culture that bears your imprint, passion, and vision and gives full expression to your coaching philosophy.

Expressed in principles, rules, habits, and style of play, your coaching philosophy defines the uniqueness of your basketball program. It is, at base, a value system of what you hold near and dear. It expresses how you love to see the game played and advances the enduring lessons you want to impart to your athletes. As you embark on the head-coaching journey, think deeply, broadly, and constantly about what you want your program to convey to players, the school, the community, and the general public.

Preliminary Coaching Philosophy Questions

You might start with these overarching questions:

1. What values do you want as the foundation of your program?
2. How do you envision the relationships between athletes and coaches, and parents and coaches?
3. What do you want the community to identify most with your program?
4. What is the learning atmosphere you envision for your teams?
5. What do see as your ideal coaching legacy?

Developing a Coaching Philosophy

There is no formula. Thoughts on what to consider follow, but appreciate they are offered merely as a guide. Your philosophy must come from within and emphasize what is important to you as the leader of the program. Prioritize and emphasize what is true to you.

1. Fundamentally, coaching is a teaching endeavor. To teach the game well, a coach must be willing to learn and grow along with the players. Players (and parents) respect coaches who display vulnerability and are open to change and personal growth.

2. An effective basketball program requires unwavering commitment to "team." For the team to succeed, the coaching staff and players must be tirelessly devoted to a common mission and have genuine respect for themselves. In this regard, the working relationship of the coaching staff is a testing ground and model for team values.

3. A basketball culture thrives on open and honest communication (see Chapter 11), in an environment where all members of the extended basketball family feel comfortable discussing matters of interest. Effective communication fosters understanding and respect, improves the quality of the experience for everyone, and, more often than not, solves problems and eliminates inaccurate perceptions.

4. Players don't care about what you know until you show them you care. Make each player feel important to the success of the team, regardless of the role you define for them.

5. We all crave affirmation, whether we admit it or not. A consistently positive culture is fun and meaningful, produces greater results, forms special bonds, and creates fond and enduring memories.

6. Relationships are the core of your program, whether with players, the AD, school administrators, teachers, parents, referees, other coaches

(inside and outside the school), or select members of the community. Keep all bridges open and intact.

7. Understand and celebrate the differences between teaching and coaching. They go hand-in-hand. The former highlights technical knowledge, the Xs and Os of what we teach. The latter encompasses the ability to transmit that knowledge effectively—how we communicate and the values we stress to our athletes—in words and actions.

8. An overarching performance standard is doing the best job possible. Everyone in a basketball program—from coach to player, parent, school administrator, and to fan—has a role to play. So long as the roles are well defined, honored, and embraced, all you can ask, at the end of the day, is that everyone do their best within those parameters.

9. If you want players to "show up" each day, you must bring it each day too. Honor the standards you set with your own consistency. Be the coach you would want to have.

10. Build trust throughout your program: trust of assistant coaches to do their job well and be honest and fair; trust of players to do what is expected of them in all aspects of the game and in the classroom and the community; and trust of parents to

support the team and coaching staff in positive ways.

11. Respect is a cornerstone value of any program, earned through actions and words.
12. Stress the intangibles that mean the most to you, (e.g., empathy, hard work, discipline, honesty, selflessness, toughness, mutual respect, and love).
13. Transparency: as much as practical, share your thinking with the players.
14. Create a culture of loyalty among coaches, between coaches and players, and among the team. Show your players you will always have their backs.
15. Under-promise, over-deliver.
16. Create an environment where fundamentals and the "little things" are valued instead of "SportsCenter" moments.
17. Exalt the principle of multiple hearts with a single heartbeat.
18. Emphasize tradition and legacy. Players have the opportunity to leave a lasting mark on the school basketball culture and inspire those who follow.

In sum, develop a system that expresses your core values and builds a culture of which the school, the community, and you can be proud.

Administrative Responsibilities

It would be nice if all coaches had to do was roll out the balls, tweet the whistle, and teach the game. But high school basketball programs include a wide range of duties beyond the game itself. The administrative components of the job add layers of time-consuming responsibilities that require a range of personal and political skills. Indeed, administrative work arguably presents the biggest challenge for the high school head coach, especially a beginner. Handling administrative responsibilities effectively will positively impact your program. Here is a summary of what to expect.

Institutional Values and Rules

For starters, as touched on in Chapter 1, you are well served to understand the institutional values of the school. Most schools have a published mission statement and expression of values. Think about how they impact your program. Straying from school values can complicate your life and, if it happens too often, risks your coaching job. In addition, be familiar with the published rules for athletics at the school, which is typically housed in an Athletic Handbook (distinguished from the Student Handbook), as well as applicable rules of your league and other private and public bodies that oversee and regulate high school basketball in your locale.

Important Relationships Outside the Gym

Know the direct chain of command and to whom you are expected to answer (in addition to the AD), including personalities and working styles. Be aware of reporting protocols, including when and how to report (e.g., a medical report when a player gets injured). When in doubt, report! Similarly, during the course of each year, situations will arise—academic, behavioral, and otherwise—that command you to speak with teachers, counselors, or other administrative personnel about specific players. Forging relationships with school professionals will enhance your ability to mentor and coach players and minimize strife.

Academics

Student-athletes have the unique duty to balance the roles of a full-time student and a dedicated athlete. The management of academic responsibilities while pursuing a demanding athletic activity requires various skills, not the least of which is time management. Each high school has mechanisms for monitoring the academic performance of its athletes and identifying looming or existing problems. In some schools, coaches rarely have to worry about such matters. In others, it is a constant focus.

A high school basketball varsity head coach functions in an educational environment and is expected to honor the preeminence of academics and the learning process. As head coach, take a genuine interest in the educational experience of your players. Get to know the faculty to the extent practical. Understand the academic performance benchmarks and monitoring system, including the rules for player eligibility and who to contact when problems come to your attention. Install your own monitoring system to stay abreast of problems as soon as or, better, *before* they arise. Strive to assure your athletes are on top of their academic responsibilities and receive necessary academic support.

Study hall, a regularly scheduled gathering of students to do homework and other classroom work, can help. Getting study halls scheduled and chaperoned can be difficult, but a regime of study hall attendance can be effective. Whether study hall is necessary or appropriate, of course, depends on the school and the specific team.

Equipment

Although athletic equipment is primarily the province of your AD, you likely will have the opportunity to influence equipment-related decisions. Understand, first, that the AD operates under budgetary constraints. This is not to say the AD lacks some discretion within the budget. It means only that because funds are limited, the AD must balance the needs and desires of an entire sports program. Still, do not be shy about advocating for what you believe your program needs. Just be realistic, diplomatic, and reasonable.

Budgets aside, when it comes to equipment, not everyone agrees on what is minimally necessary, important, and extravagant. Mindful that reasonable people might differ on what is basic equipment and what is not, here are two lists to consider.

Basic items might include:

- At least 15 relatively new basketballs and sufficient ball carts
- Modern uniforms, including shooting shirts, and warm up outfits
- An electric air pump
- Player travel and ball bags

- Reversible practice jerseys and scrimmage vests ("jimmies")
- Basketball shoes
- Water bottles and cooler
- Clipboards
- Fully stocked medical kit
- Cones or other floor markers
- Coaching whistles
- Large white board in team meeting room(m) Film projector equipment
- Pads (karate-style) for bumping players during lay-up and how drills

Non-basic items might include:

- Training and conditioning equipment (e.g., agility ladders, training or "heavy" balls, and jump ropes)
- Shooting machine or other shooting aids
- Rebounding aids
- Floor tape
- Traction mats
- Compression sleeves
- Ballhandling goggles and gloves
- Custom mouth guards
- Resister bands
- Plyometric and speed training equipment

Scheduling

Scheduling is a bright star in the constellation of head coaching duties and deserves its own chapter. See Chapter 5.

Transportation

The school will have a system and set of rules for team transportation. For example, the rules might establish conditions under which coaches may drive players to and from games (if at all), whether driving-licensed players may drive other players, the conditions under which parents may drive players (typically with auto insurance minimums), and whether players must travel to games on school-supplied transportation but can return with parents (or other adults). This is not an area for fudging. Be clear on how transportation works at your school and abide. As discussed in Chapter 12, consider anointing a parent volunteer the Transportation Czar to coordinate all travel for the team. It is a headache you will be happy to delegate.

Fundraising

The importance of fundraising, especially when operating under limited budgets for equipment and activities, cannot be overstated. Rules that govern fundraising, however, differ by school. Some do not permit any. Some permit fundraising within specified parameters, like through professional fundraisers. The governing rules can be complicated. Be prepared to take advantage of whatever is allowed for your program. Most basketball programs can use extra funds.

If permitted, think about a program- or team-specific bank account where you maintain funds from independent sources either through fundraising or contributions from the community. Such an account can supplement what the school provides and help families in financial need.

Team Outings

Team building activities, like off-campus outings, are an integral part of a sports program. They enliven community spirit, break down barriers between players, refine relationships, and develop leadership skills. They also advance program values such as collective accomplishment and team chemistry, effective communication, emphasis on role, reliability, positivity, and trust.

The market contains many options for team building activities. Investigate them to identify experiences well suited for what you are trying to build. Planning for them should begin early, before the season if possible. Fitting these activities into the schedule, obtaining the necessary funds, as well as making sure you complete requisite paperwork and obtain necessary approvals, requires time and effort.

Booster Clubs

The existence of an active and supportive booster organization can be manna. While not every school has
a booster club, those that do provide attractive opportunities to get funds for items not otherwise available
or difficult to obtain, like team-building activities and
non-basic equipment. They can also supply financial
support to families of players in need. Be diplomatic.
Identify the persons in the booster club who are enthusiastic about your program and develop relationships
with them.

General Community

To state the obvious, it is easier to fill seats for games if
the "product" you put on the floor is exciting. Conversely,
generating community support when the product is
not so thrilling can be more difficult. Regardless, there
are ways to drum up community support. For example, invite local middle school, CYO, AAU, and other
club teams to your practices and games. Offer to speak
to these groups. Put on clinics and use your players in
them. Entice people to games with contests. Market
the annual alumni game to increase program exposure
and build community spirit. Explore with your AD—
and the booster club if you have one—how to increase
community support. Be creative. Make the community
a priority.

Media

You may or may not have much opportunity to speak to the media during the season. In some jurisdictions, for example, it is common for local papers to interview coaches after each game, typically the coach on the winning side, to get game stats and game perspectives. In addition, local papers will sometimes do feature stories on certain players and will seek your comment. Local papers might preview upcoming league competition and will look to league head coaches for input. And, every now and then controversy arises, which prompts the media to come calling for comment. If you have the opportunity to deal with the media, keep the following in mind:

1. Embrace the media; they are not the enemy. They have an important job to do for the community and can bring positive attention to your program and players. Be lighthearted and they will respond in kind. Deep down, they want to be associated with you.

2. Get to know your main media contacts early. While they will not admit it, they don't like all coaches; if they like and respect you, you will get better treatment.

3. The media is an opportunity to continue the messages and values you advance every day with the team, parents, and the school community.

4. Be prepared. Anticipate questions as best you can and formulate preliminary answers.

5. Where applicable, keep them in the loop and, where appropriate, have an understanding about what can and cannot be printed. They thrive on being informed early and often.

6. Understand your real audience. You are talking with the media but speaking to the public, which includes your team, specific players sometimes, parents, and the school, among others. What do you want *them* to read? As a general guide, be positive and constructive. Praise and criticism each go a long way, but in different directions. And remember: less is more!

7. On a related point, pay close attention to the difference between what you *intend* by your words and the likely *impact* of your words. Again, think through how players, parents, other coaches, and your AD might react to specific comments from *their* vantage points.

8. Be relaxed, but not so relaxed you are glib or prone to use slang. If during the interview you realize you said something you regret, more often than not, the interviewer will dump the quote.

9. Dealing with the media will enhance your communication skills. Find your own media voice. Be yourself in how you deal with the media.

10. Be digitally savvy. Your players will be on social media incessantly. Make sure they fully appreciate the importance of being smart—meaning discrete—about what they post on social media. And, for your part, keep your social media PRIVATE!
11. If you feel uncomfortable answering a question, simply say you prefer not to answer.
12. Make sure you know when the school expects you to check first before agreeing to an interview. This typically arises when the press is investigating an incident.

Relationships with Other Coaches

Lastly, while not an administrative matter, developing camaraderie with coaches in your league and beyond will enhance your overall coaching experience and also reap benefits, including obtaining game film for scouting purposes. Especially from coaches who are substantially more experienced, get their counsel on the challenges you face. Seek your colleagues out before games to chat. Coaches generally feel a special bond with other coaches.

Assistant Varsity Coaches

The value of assistant coaches is immeasurable. The successful implementation of a high school basketball program requires a comprehensive team effort no different than what is required to win basketball games. The hiring of the right assistants—ideally at least two—is essential.

Hopefully, you will have the final word on selection of your assistants (as well as direct say in the hiring of the lower level team coaches in your program). If not, you should work diplomatically toward getting control over assistant hires. Other than your AD, they are your most important relationships and who they are should reflect what matters to you.

Difficulty arises when assistants from the old regime want to stay. Retaining them is tempting. It avoids the angst of saying "no thanks" and the sometimes arduous process of replacing them. As easy as it might be to re-tain them, however, you owe it to yourself and the pro-gram to undertake an independent assessment and job search. Most ADs will support this approach. Hire the coaches you believe are best for *your* program, all things considered (as discussed below). Don't settle! It is too important a decision.

Budget plays a role here. Schools, especially public, are stingy in allocating funds for assistants, which can make the search for the right persons thorny at best. This often means tapping into the volunteer market, which is particularly tough if you want to hire young assistants (who need cash flow to live). Some varsity coaches share their paltry salaries with assistants to assure a reliable coaching staff. Where there's a will...

The Search

Identify the most effective ways to find assistants. The school will help with customary advertisements in lo-cal papers and on websites. Job postings at local col-leges and on athletic websites can be fruitful. Craigslist also can be a rich source of potential candidates and is worth the modest fee to see what an ad brings.

Word of mouth also can be a fertile source. Reach out to the community of coaches and ADs (provided they are not competing to hire). They might produce poten-tial candidates who are tried, true, and trusted.

Interview Process and References

The assistant coach interview process tends to be informal. After initial contact, meet with candidates, one on one. Your AD will let you know whether they need to meet them and, if so, it typically is a formality. If you are happy with someone, and the candidate looks good on paper and does not give anyone pause, subject to reference checks, your AD should be good to go.

Selection Criteria

Establish criteria for *your* ideal assistant coach. Each criterion might not be indispensable, but the list will provide an excellent barometer for the interview process and decisions. Here are suggestions.

1. Does the candidate have sufficient prior (coaching and playing) experience to perform the role you have in mind? In other words, does the candidate have the technical and tactical skills and seasoning you require?

2. Are you satisfied—after an open discussion—the candidate will be steadfastly loyal to you?

3. Does the candidate *appear* to be a solid citizen and possess the intangibles you like (e.g., integrity, honesty beyond reproach, trustworthiness, respectfulness, work ethic, punctuality, and program commitment)?

4. Does the candidate have a genuine willingness to perform the role as *you* define it?

5. Does the candidate have a natural passion for the game?

6. Does the candidate exude enthusiasm for coaching and selfless devotion to student-athletes?

7. Is the candidate likely to be a proper role model for players?

8. Do the candidate's expressed coaching goals fit your program vision?

9. Does the candidate seem comfortable presenting a different opinion than yours and promoting new ideas and equally understand the time, place, and manner for sharing them?

10. Was the candidate prepared at the interview and comfortable asking questions?

11. Is the candidate's personality a good fit (i.e., a balance) with yours and what the program needs?

12. Does the candidate appear approachable to players and someone who understands the broad line between coach and player?

13. How are candidate's communication skills?

14. Do the candidate's non-coaching commitments harmonize with the time commitment you expect of an assistant?

15. Is the candidate someone you would enjoy in social interactions outside the gym?

Assistant Coach Roles and Tasks

Head coaching tests your willingness and ability to delegate and smartly define roles for others. The long list of coaching tasks is beyond what any head coach can handle. Head coaches need help in almost every facet of the job. Organizing coaching staff roles, with clear and embraced expectations, eases pressure and makes for a more effective program. Here is a litany of tasks to consider for your staff, noting that some apply to all assistants and others contemplate individual role assignments.

1. Provide regular input on player development.
2. Report all conversations with players and parents regarding all aspects of the program.
3. Help in all aspects of tryouts, including player selection.
4. Help prepare practices and, when requested, run drills.
5. Set up and close the gym for practices, including bringing baskets down and ready for use, bringing out anticipated equipment, sweeping the floor, and having water or other hydration ready for the team. (Doubtless, you will share in some or all of this.)
6. Share observations during practices (via sidebars).
7. Make suggestions about player roles, practice drills, and offensive and defensive sets, but

privately; in other words, your assistants should not negotiate changes with you in front of the team.

8. Help scout and film opponents and break down film. (See Chapter 18).

9. Bring a fully stocked medical kit and set of warm-up balls to away games and collect them during and after games.

10. If necessary, keep game statistics.

11. Have the dry erase board available during time-outs.

12. Handle some or all of the following game responsibilities:

   • Bring a list of the other team's most and least reliable foul shooters.

   • Track the fouls and time-outs of both teams and monitor the possession arrow (and remind players as need be).

   • Look out for when the other team is about to call time-out (and thus possibly save one of your own).

   • Make sure the team on the floor assembles during dead ball situations.

   • Handle substitutions (if you delegate this task) and monitor the other team's substitutions.

   • Confer with players during game situations on the bench, especially players who have just come off the floor.

- Monitor players for fatigue.
- Remind players when they may run the baseline after a make.
- Monitor defensive matchups.
- Speak to the team on your cue during halftime or after a game.
- Participate in postgame coach debriefings.

Meetings

Like most head coaches, you will have conversations with assistants once or more each day during the season. Equally important, however, are off-site meetings for expanded discussions on team progress, upcoming challenges, program direction, and individual player evaluations. These meetings foster improved coaching and enhanced coaching relationships and often produce great ideas.

The contours and specifics of the relationship between you and your assistants are unique to your program. They are an expression of your vision and collaborative values. Cherish the opportunities to build something with trusted colleagues.

Scheduling the Season – Games and Practices

The season schedule is the coaching analog of a business plan, and is part science and part art. The science part concerns immovable objects, like various rules that limit your discretion and school events that block out days. The art component springs from creatively devising a schedule that advances your short- and long-term vision for the program.

League games are out of your control, except to the extent you have general input on scheduling in annual league meetings (e.g., regarding when to start league competition or what days of the week to set aside for league games) and in the rare circumstance when scheduling complications arise regarding a particular league game.

In most schools, the head coach controls the preseason game schedule. As a new head coach, however, you might need to log a couple years of experience learning the scheduling ropes and building confidence with your AD before getting full control of those reigns. The practice schedule, discussed at the end of this chapter, is another matter. Depending on when you are hired relative to the start of the season, the schedule your first year might be set. If it is, you go with it. If not, you get to work.

Games and Scrimmages

When to Start Scheduling. The time to embark on the scheduling journey—and it can be a journey—is as soon as practical after the prior season ends. You are competing for the time of others and battling steadily decreasing options. Schedules fill up fast, and the sooner you focus on nailing down dates, the better the prospects of getting the schedule you prefer. You may have to juggle a little, negotiate dates, times and locations, and even revisit original commitments when problems arise. It can be a fluid situation. Start right away!

Scheduling Limitations. Before devising your scheduling plan, know where your hands are tied or options limited. For example:

1. By rule, there will be a maximum number of games, counting league games (typically *exclusive* of playoff games), that may be played before

postseason competition begins. This includes a maximum number of scrimmages.

2. Certain days, also by rule, are not available for games. Your school might, for example, forbid games on certain holidays and during exam week. While winter break is a fertile opportunity for tournaments and games, be sure that period is open season. Applicable government rules might forbid games on Sundays. Know all the dark days before you get rolling.

3. If practical, have the league schedule in mind. If it is not ready by the time you start, know at least the first day of league competition (e.g., January 4) and the days of the week the league schedules games (e.g., Tuesdays, Thursdays, and Saturdays). Hopefully, you won't need to schedule a preseason game during league, but, as discussed in the next section, it can happen.

4. Be aware of any travel restrictions the school imposes. You might not be permitted to travel certain distances, or to certain areas or schools.

5. Sometimes the constraints of scheduling might force you to consider back-to-back preseason games. While hardly ideal, and should generally be avoided, it can happen.

6. Generally, while it is easy to get lost in scheduling details, stay true to how the school defines

success and what you want for the values of the program you are building.

Game Selection Criteria. There are many factors to weigh in deciding how to construct a preseason scheduling plan, depending on short- and long-term program goals. Ask four threshold questions: (1) where is your program now and where do you think you can take it, (2) what is the current state of player and team skills (and DNA), (3) what is the landscape of your competition, and (4) for the current season, are you more focused on league competition, postseason competition, a *relatively* rewarding first campaign regardless of the end result, or some of each?

The answers to those questions are your planning framework. Plan strategically what schools to play and when to play them. Consider the specifics that follow, as you seek to strike a balance that works for you.

7. *Scrimmages.* As noted, rules limit allowable scrimmages during the season, typically two. The threshold consideration is when to schedule them. Scrimmages are effective opportunities to get teams ready to start the preseason. If that is how you want to use scrimmages, try to schedule them within the first two weeks of the season— before the first preseason game (if practical). Alternatively, you may want to use a scrimmage as a tune-up shortly before league competition starts.

8. *Charity Game.* Many jurisdictions urge a charity game on a set day, which may not count against the maximum allowable games. If so, it is an opportunity for what is effectively another scrimmage.

9. *Road Games.* Road games during the preseason can help prepare your team for adverse conditions. The more of them you schedule, the more challenging the preseason. On the other hand, if you have a senior-laden team, you might consider a heavy tilt toward home games to ease the separate burden of college visits and applications.

10. *Postseason "Seeding."* If your postseason system ranks or seeds teams for postseason competition, as most do, note that seeding criteria typically favor head-to-head results. Consider therefore planning preseason games against opponents or common opponents of opponents you likely will vie against for postseason seeding position.

11. *Ws.* To what extent do you want preseason games you assume your team will win? Most coaches stage a few and some more. It depends on your short- and long-term goals. (*See* next paragraph.)

12. *Competitive Challenges.* Everyone schedules tough games to challenge their teams and get them ready for league and post-league competition. The question is how many to schedule. Be wary of games against vastly superior teams, for the

impact might not be what you want. Also, if you are in a rebuilding mode or have taken over a program with a history of little or no recent success, you might want to balance the need for competitive games against the need to give the team the taste of winning.

13. *Targeted Upsets and "Reminder" Games.* While a gamble, you might want to schedule some games against teams against which a win would constitute a noteworthy upset. Even if you can't get the upset, that kind of game can serve as a measure of what the team needs to get done.

14. *Home and Away Customs.* When you get hired, your school might have existing customs with certain schools for alternating home and away preseason games. It can be a worthy custom. The flip side occurs if one of you has regressed substantially, rendering the game no longer competitive. Whether to retain the custom weighs the historical relationship against what is best for your team.

15. *Divisional Games.* Many high school systems have tiered competitive levels in the form of divisions, typically based on enrollment size. Be cautious of—but not necessarily averse to—scheduling "down." A loss to a lower division team in preseason can hurt your postseason seeding.

16. *Overlapping Preseason and League Schedule.* Sometimes it is too difficult to schedule all

preseason games before the onset of league competition. This means scheduling a preseason game during the period reserved for league competition, providing the rules allow that to happen (or to the extent they do). Rather than fall short of maximum games allowed, it is usually better to squeeze a preseason game into the league season, often on a Saturday in lieu of a practice.

17. *Different Styles of Play.* Another way to increase the competitive experience is scheduling games against teams with varied styles of play (e.g., pressing, zone or transition, or three-point shooting teams).

18. *Fun Venues.* Similarly, consider a fun venue or two (e.g., schools that pack gyms regularly) where an exciting atmosphere is assured.

19. *Tournaments.* Tournaments raise various thoughts. Do you, for example, schedule one or two? Do you prefer commuter or overnight (or both)? Do you prefer them late in the preseason, like over the winter break (which is typical), at other times (e.g., early December), or both? Are there any financial and academic considerations? Do you select tournaments your predecessor favored or do you change it up? What can you learn in advance about the likely tournament competition and how it jives with your overall preseason plan?

20. *League Opponents.* Some schools wind up in tournaments with league opponents. Before joining such a tournament, weigh the impact of playing a league opponent before the onset of league competition, win or lose, against the benefits of the particular tournament.
21. *Double and Triple Headers.* Depending on the number of teams in your program, one goal is to schedule double (varsity and JV) or triple (varsity, JV and frosh, or frosh/soph) headers. They are fun and help build program spirit and camaraderie.
22. *Formulae.* Some coaches employ a formula to prepare the preseason schedule (e.g., 40 percent anticipated Ws, 40 percent toss-up games, and 20 percent games looking for upsets).
23. *Games Wanted Sites.* Finally, if all else fails, know that various websites have a section for "games wanted," where you can search for games and post your own wants and desires.

No matter what your approach, be politely persistent with other coaches. Operate by the idiom "the squeaky wheel gets the grease." After the season, coaches retreat to their other lives and sometimes, excuse the pun, drop the ball. Stay on them to get the game schedule you want. Also, create a regularly updated spreadsheet with contact information for coaches and ADs for use every year.

One final note: transparency in game scheduling is important. Let your team and parents know what you are trying to accomplish with the schedule you put together. Sometimes game selection confuses them. Better they know your thinking than otherwise.

Practice Schedule

The practice schedule implicates many, sometimes conflicting, factors (e.g., other hoops teams [as many as five] competing for limited gym time; whether there is one or two gyms; school and community events in the gym that take precedence over the basketball program; and, applicable rules that limit practice hours per week or mandate days you are not permitted to practice).

Your AD presides over the practice schedule. You should, however, have an opportunity to sit down with the AD and presumably the other varsity basketball coach to work things out. A face-to-face meeting among the three of you is an excellent way to work through all issues and fairly consider all relevant factors. Here are factors to ponder.

Times and Frequency. Most programs permit teams to practice each day, except Sunday, and most varsity teams take advantage of this policy. Bear in mind that practice time, once games begin, becomes increasingly precious. Getting the team into the gym at each opportunity is important. The harder question is when after school to practice. You may have to negotiate this with the AD and other varsity coach. For example, your AD might, understandably, be reluctant to have lower level teams practicing late and prefer the varsity teams to take most, if not all, the late slots. Another consideration is practicing the same or near the time your team plays its games, which has the benefit of familiarity. Your own non-coaching obligations might be a factor too, as well as your assistants' schedules. Further, the lower level coaches will have their own schedule wish list. A viable solution is alternating time slots. There is also the option, which surprisingly many players (but not all parents!) favor, of some morning practices (e.g., 6 a.m.), which frees up after-school slots. In the end, it is a matter of finding balance and being fair.

Thanksgiving, Exam Week, and Winter Break. Most varsity teams, to the chagrin of some families, practice over the Thanksgiving weekend and during winter and other extended school breaks, albeit at different times of the day than the regular schedule. Schools are sometimes reluctant to make practices mandatory for lower level teams during some of these periods, but varsity teams have greater leeway. Schools may have rules prohibiting practices during exam week or make them voluntary or operated as "open gyms." Know your options.

Game Shootarounds. If you have the luxury of an extra gym, grabbing time in the second facility before home games for a pregame shootaround is ideal, whenever it is a realistic scheduling option. Players relish extra shooting work, including foul shots, before a game. It is also an opportunity to review game preparation and walk through planned offensive sets, inbounds plays, defensive rotations, and strategy, among other things. Don't wait for game week to see if the space is available. Try to get access—and thus priority—before the season unfolds.

Tryouts

Tryouts mark a new dawn, a rebirth, like the beginning of spring, as the first days of the season burst with exhilaration, hope, and the promise of potential. Tryouts also bring pervasive anxiety and worry, from players hoping to make the grade, to coaches who might turn away some athletes, and to parents fretting about how their child will fare in this latest challenge. As a result, there is a different kind of buzz in the gym during tryouts. Freeze the special moment. There is much to consider in this dynamic context.

Pre-Tryouts Meeting

Consider a pre-tryouts informational meeting at the school for all candidates for all program teams a week or two before the first day of tryouts. The meeting might include:

1. The tryouts schedule.
2. An overview of team selection criteria and what candidates can expect during tryouts.
3. The importance of candidates playing within themselves at tryouts and not obsessing or over-focusing on proving themselves.
4. If applicable, the reality of cuts, how many players each team will *likely* carry and how you will communicate decisions.
5. Reminders about grade point eligibility and medical or other requirements. (Note: work closely with administrative staff to monitor who is—and who is not—eligible to tryout).
6. A sign-up sheet to collect names, email addresses, school year, and what team each player aspires to make (often revealing information).

Tryouts Preparation

Like everything else, tryouts must be planned well. To start, although you will be free to craft your own tryout plan, it might help to know how the school has handled tryouts previously. For example, historically, has everyone tried out at the same time? JV and frosh together? Freshman separately? Does your AD expect you to hold tryouts during a set period (e.g., two or three days) or is it left to you? Typically, varsity tryouts take less time than JV or freshmen.

Meet in advance with your staff to organize tryouts. Drills should reflect the criteria for selecting players. For example, if conditioning is a factor (see below), pepper tryouts with conditioning drills. If you want to see how well they defend on-the-ball, use of 3-on-3 competition or one-on-one full court can effectively test them. The list can go on.

Also, what role do you prefer to play in tryouts? While it may be tempting to sit back and observe, if it is your first rodeo, you need to establish your presence and program leadership. Nonetheless, you will want some time to observe with a fine eye, so consider having assistants run some drills.

Allocate time to discuss with the coaching staff what you learn during tryouts. While sidebars among coaches during tryouts will occur, you will need focused quiet time after each session to compare notes. Keep always in mind that you are making impactful decisions.

Selection Criteria

Be specific about selection criteria and how you prioritize the list. The criteria can include, among other things:

7. Emotional and mental readiness for high school competition.

8. The ever-important intangibles: positive and supportive attitude (team player qualities), work ethic, ability to follow instructions, coachability, punctuality, competitive spirit, maturity, and discipline.

9. Love of the game (basketball-first player).

10. Physicality.

11. Basketball fundamentals.

12. Range and depth of specific skills.

13. Appropriate knowledge of the game or "basketball IQ."

14. Long-term potential. Sometimes a candidate for a lower level team has underdeveloped and limited skills but possesses significant upside potential for the program, (e.g., a Big). If push came to shove and you had to choose, in what circumstance would you favor that player over one with greater current skills?

15. Conditioning.

16. Leadership skills.

Decision-Making Process

As you gain experience, you will quickly know where you stand with most candidates, either because you have seen them in competitive situations before or it becomes obvious relatively soon. At some point during tryouts, it is important to get a handle on which players are on the bubble so the coaching staff can pay more attention to them. Players shrouded in uncertainty deserve more attention than others.

The final decisions are yours, for that is where the buck stops. But perhaps to state the obvious, a consensus approach is best. Sure, if you cannot convince your staff about someone, you should be free to make the decision notwithstanding their dissent. But unanimity is preferred, particularly for the tough calls. It is worth repeating that it is vital to have continuing dialogue among the coaching staff during tryouts and meetings after each day of tryouts to share perceptions and refine the decision-making process.

Underclassmen and Tryouts

Whether to place lower classmen on upper teams (e.g., a freshman on varsity) in the absence of an ironclad prohibition, can be a tough decision.

1. The overriding considerations are whether the player is likely to get substantial playing time and whether placing that player on a higher team might hamper the intellectual, emotional, and physical development that might otherwise occur on the lower team. Skilled players not accustomed to the stress and physicality of varsity play might need grounding at a lower level before "playing up." There is a marked difference between dominating eighth grade competition and competing at the varsity level, including landing

in a different and often unfamiliar place in the team hierarchy.

2. Consider, too, whether placing a freshman on varsity will make academic adjustments from middle school to high school more difficult. Academic loads in high school tend to dwarf what must be carried in middle school. The pressure and time commitment of varsity competition might make it more difficult for some freshmen to carry the load effectively.

3. On the other hand, depending on the player, a talented youngster may not be sufficiently challenged playing at the lower level. If held back as it were, player morale might suffer, as well as athletic growth. A freshman player who is ready for prime time, physically, emotionally, and academically, might be developmentally harmed if excluded from a more competitive environment, also to the detriment of the varsity team.

4. Some coaches have a strict rule: no freshmen on varsity, regardless. The benefit is that expectations are clear from the go, no matter how skilled or star-studded a player entering high school. The underlying message is that players must earn the privilege of playing at the top level over the course of at least one high school season, if not more.

5. In the end, this type of decision should turn, fundamentally, on what is best for the athlete. The

interests of the program, while important, should be secondary.

Returning Players

Consider a policy about whether returning varsity players have an automatic spot or must, like everyone else, make the grade in tryouts. This can be especially dicey for returning seniors who are on the cusp. Understand that no matter how structured and transparent your decision-making process, if you cut a returning player, especially a senior, political fallout is likely and you may need the AD to have your back. Be thoughtful and make sure your process is fair, including giving returning players advance notice when they are at risk of not making the grade. This is not to say you should or should not cut such players, only that their situations require thought and sensitivity.

Communicating Tryout Decisions

Getting cut hurts. Sometimes there are tears; sometimes anger. Most coaches find the process personally challenging. The anticipated player anguish can make it difficult to discuss cut decisions with players. If, however, coaches handle the process openly, thoughtfully, and respectfully, they are standing up for important values. Identify situations where you should coordinate with the AD about tryouts, especially tough decisions with potential for political fallout (as discussed earlier).

The better practice is to communicate selections and cuts one-on-one in person. Emails or posting lists on the wall are impersonal and disrespectful. All candidates, whether selected or not, deserve a personal meeting—they had the courage to tryout and coaches can have the courage to look them in the eye and tell them how they fared. This can happen during the last day of tryouts while drills are ongoing. You can pull players aside quietly and briefly communicate your decision and offer to meet at greater length another time to discuss the decision in depth.

Wrapping Up Tryouts

There are housekeeping details to handle after tryouts.

1. The coaching staff should thank everyone who tried out for their effort. Students not chosen for teams can be encouraged to assume team-related roles such as team manager, scorekeeper, and statistician. They typically decline—egos rising—but every now and then you land someone who knows the game and can be helpful.

2. Hold a brief meeting with the newly constituted varsity (as your other coaches should do with the lower level teams) to make an initial connection, congratulate everyone, and discuss a few details, like upcoming practices and the team potluck (see Chapter 7).

3. Get email addresses for players and family adults.
    This should be done right away, if not already
    done before tryouts.

You're Not Done Yet: Candidates in
Overlapping Seasonal Sports

Depending on your jurisdiction, you might be prevented from closing tryouts officially pending the conclusion of another sport still underway from the prior
athletic season, like football or cross-country. This
means keeping tryouts open until players participating
in those other sports have the opportunity to tryout,
which normally is not permitted until the other sports
team has concluded its season. In most cases, where
the impacted athletes are no-brainers, there is no problem. Where doubt exists, however, and you are firm in
how many players you want to carry, you have a bit of
a dilemma.

If you leave a slot (or more) open, you have to cut
players you otherwise would take if you were allocating
all the slots. If players from other sports fail to make
the grade, you either have fewer players than you want
or must rescind earlier cuts. Of course, if players from
the other sport make the team, you have dodged that
bullet.

If you fill every spot, and a player from the other
sport makes the team, you have to carry one player

more than you wanted. But if that player fails to make the team, you are right where you want to be.

A third alternative is not leaving any slot open, but telling everyone tryouts shall remain open until players in the other spots tryout; in other words, team selection is *provisional*. The vice in this approach is that you don't control when the other sport ends and, when it does, you may have to cut a player who was on the team for weeks, has a uniform, played in a scrimmage and maybe even a game, and attended (with family) the kickoff potluck (see Chapter 7).

The prudent course seems to pick the full team the first time out. The final player chosen earned the right to make the team based on the totality of competition during the scheduled tryout sessions. Players from other sports with uncertain prospects can take their chances. If any wows you, better you carry an extra player than endure those alternative scenarios. A variation on this approach, if you are committed to a precise number of team members, is to deem certain players provisionally accepted after group tryouts, which means those provisionally accepted players are effectively competing for remaining slots directly with those players who try out arrive after the season for the other sport is over.

Season-Kickoff Potluck

Once the team is selected, it is a great idea to hold a potluck for the team and their families at the earliest practical time after tryouts, ideally the next weekend. The potluck is a special opportunity to set the tone for the season and create community spirit among the larger family for the team journey, introduce (or re-introduce) yourself and your staff, lay the groundwork for program expectations and provide and collect information.

If by this time you have team parents lined up (see Chapter 8), they can handle organizing the event. If not, it falls to you, hopefully with some parent help, to get it organized. In either case:

1. Pick a day and a time (e.g., the first Sunday after tryouts from, say, 1–3 or 4–6, works for virtually all if not all families). You might, before tryouts,

want to send out a save-the-date email to secure
a date and time.

2. Get a family to volunteer their home or, alternatively, find a school-approved location on campus
   to use.

3. Assign families what to bring (e.g., appetizers,
   beverages, entrees, dessert, etc.).

4. Think about whom else to invite, like the school
   trainer if you have one or academic counselor, to
   speak briefly about how they support the team.

Once logistics are handled, be prepared at the potluck
to discuss your program, particularly what lies in store
for everyone. The following is suggestive:

1. Thank everyone for coming and give special
   thanks to all who contributed to the event.

2. Introduce coaches, other professionals in attendance, and, if determined by that point, the team
   parent(s).

3. Summarize your background and experience.

4. Provide an overview of your vision and expectations for the program, including for the upcoming
   season.

5. Promote a family atmosphere for your program.

6. Review your coaching philosophy, and team rules
   and goals.

7. Identify the player intangibles important to you
   (e.g., honesty, punctuality, work ethic, loyalty,
   team-first attitude, positivity, and so on).

8. Discuss practice expectations and review the practice schedule.

9. Discuss how players can earn "playing time," better described as "opportunities to contribute (OTC)," stressing that OTC is not a right but an earned privilege.

10. Review the scrimmage, game, and tournament schedule. As discussed in Chapter 5, explain your game selections generally so they know your thinking.

11. Highlight the program values of special importance to you, e.g., self-advocacy (players taking initiative to raise issues directly with coaches rather than parents)

12. Discuss the school's hierarchal protocol for initiating contact with you (i.e., when players should approach the coach directly, when parents may approach the coach, and when parents may approach the AD).

13. Describe guidelines for game day, including how you expect parents to behave at games (positive cheering, not putting down other players, no yelling at the referees, no criticizing coaches, and absolutely no sideline coaching). Explain that there is no talking to you on game days about any issues (because of the flood of emotion in those circumstances).

14. Discuss, gently, your vision of the parental role in the program and how parents can contribute

positively; in other words, diplomatically draw some lines between parent and coach.

15. If applicable, discuss fundraising and the booster club.

16. Present ideas you have for team outings (e.g., ropes course, community volunteer work, college basketball game, and so on).

17. If inclined, get buy-in on holding team dinners before certain home games and get volunteers to host.

18. Have sign-up sheets for other game responsibilities including drivers for away games; chaperones for away tournament(s); filming games; bringing water and snacks to games; handling the scorebook (for at least away games assuming the school provides someone for home games); and recording game statistics.

19. Get suggestions from parents and players on potential team managers.

20. Answer any questions.

The seasonal-kickoff potluck helps set the stage for everything that follows in the program. Approach it with the same diligence, care, and sensitivity you do other program matters.

Front Line Support — Team Parents and Manager

If you will forgive a cliché that might be a tad worn, it takes a village to operate an effective and meaningful high school basketball program. This includes, as listed in Chapter 7, an array of volunteers to perform various specific activities. The front line, however, the people who will make a noticeable difference in the life of your program, and who will make your life immeasurably better, are team parents and a team manager.

Team Parents

Team parents are integral and worthy of canonization. It is hard to imagine a program without them. You want one—and preferably two—motivated, enthusiastic, and diligent parents effectively to join your staff. They will make your daily life better and improve the quality of your program. They are invaluable.

Finding Team Parents. Finding one team parent, never mind two, is not always easy. The team parent role is time-consuming and difficult—and parents tend to have full lives. No matter when you get the head coaching job, however, make it a priority. Find out who filled the role the year before. While they might not want a repeat engagement or be available, they can make suggestions. Get suggestions also from the AD, who will know the families. If you are hired early enough, you can canvass parents during the summer program (see Chapter 21). If desperation begins to ooze, pull out the stops and poll individual parents. Sometimes parents are willing to help if they have a partner with whom to share the burden. Enlist one to entice another. Make it hard to say no! Be charmingly insistent.

1. *Team Parent Responsibilities.* Once team parents are on board, meet with them to review their responsibilities and how they can contribute to a rewarding season. Stress they are free to delegate various responsibilities. Here is a suggested job description.

2. *Role Models.* Above all, they should strive to be positive role models for other parents, especially during games. This can challenge them in

situations where they need to intervene to address negative parent behavior. It is something to monitor closely with them.

3. *Potluck.* If they sign up before tryouts, they can coordinate the potluck. Don't expect them to volunteer their home, although if they are up for it, so much the better.

4. *Contact List.* Have them create (if you have not already) a team contact list with names of players and parents, mobile and home phone numbers, and email addresses. It might also include a phone or email tree set up.

5. *Game Scorebook.* While ideally suited for a team manager (see below), an important task for team parents is lining up people to handle the game scorebook. Not everyone can do this job. It can be learned, and if that is necessary, you go with it. But you prefer someone who understands the game at a basic level. The school might provide someone independent of your group for home games, meaning you only need someone for away games, including tournaments. It does not have to be the same person—alternating with another is fine. Once the book folks are in place, meet with them to discuss how you want to book filled, including how to tally final game numbers.

6. *Transportation.* Unless the school provides transportation in the form of a van or bus, you will

need drivers for away games, via carpooling. Team parents can handle this or possibly find one parent—the Transportation Czar—who can be solely responsible for all transportation. This is an important undertaking. As game time approaches, the last thing you want is a frantic call from a player who, for whatever reason, does not have a ride to the game.

7. *Chaperones.* As noted, in addition to drivers, overnight tournaments require chaperones to supervise players during non-basketball activities.

8. *Game Filming.* Film your games. The challenge is getting parents to film since, understandably, they want to watch the game. In addition, some parents are more adept at filming than others. You can minimize the burden by having two parents film a half each. Your team parents can figure all this out.

9. *Game Statistics.* You will need someone to record game statistics—accurately! Again, this is ideally suited for a team manager. But if that is not an option, you will need parent volunteers who know the game. You especially want to see the stats at halftime before addressing the team. In a pinch, an assistant coach can handle.

10. *Snack Bar.* If your school has a snack bar at home games, team parents should organize the

requisite staffing in coordination with the other varsity team.

11. *Game Hydration.* Similarly, someone needs to be on top of hydration for the players at games. This does not have to be a team parent or any parent for that matter. It can be the team manager, should you be so lucky to have one, or an assistant coach. Alternatively, distribute assigned water bottles to the players, which puts the onus on them. Do whatever works best.

12. *Team Dinners.* If practical, team dinners during the season before certain games are an effective way to build team camaraderie and spirit for the impending game. Team parents can identify parents to host. They can also take place on campus.

13. *Postseason Party.* As virtually all teams do, hold a party after the season to wrap things up, give awards, and so on, which team parents can organize. (See Chapter 21.)

As is plain, the team parent job is comprehensive, although the burden is lessened with delegation, which also fosters inclusion. Even though team parents will keep you informed and let you focus on other stuff, meet with them from time to time to make sure all is well and shower them with the kudos they deserve.

Team Manager

Finding a team manager can be difficult. Students who are cut typically decline the opportunity and getting a busy student to step up is tough. Another option is a recently graduated student or former player who is taking a gap year. Of course, finding someone is substantially easier if you can get funds for the position. Another thought is seeking out an intern from a local college who wants exposure to the coaching experience and the ins and outs of a high school basketball program. Contact local colleges with internships to see whether their programs have options that could work for you.

If you are fortunate to land someone (or, even better, two people!), you can allocate some assistant coach and team parent duties to the team manager (e.g., setting up the gym, minding the balls and medical kit at games, handling game statistics, making sure players have the correct water bottles in games, handling the scorebook, and so on). You can define the job to fit your needs and the strengths, preferences, and agreed-upon time commitment of the team manager.

Goal Setting

Everyone has goals for whatever they do, implied or express. Goals propel us forward, providing sustained focus and motivation. They render challenges manageable and help prioritize what is important. They can inspire us to believe in ourselves and hold us accountable. They can enhance organizational and time management skills.

Setting goals is especially important for high school athletes, an important habit that, once ingrained, will be with them for all time. Consider embedding goal setting in the foundation of your basketball program. Specific goals, which typically, but not always, are measurable, need not be etched in stone; they can fluctuate as experience mounts, information flows, and circumstances change.

It starts with you. Coaches owe themselves a duty to formulate their own goals to establish goal setting as a genuine and an enduring value of the program.

Coaching Goals

Coaching goals should reflect what you realistically want to achieve as a coach. They can run the gamut including the goals of the entire coaching staff, individual coaching goals, or a combination of both. Get with your assistants and create a list that works for everyone. There is no judgment in this process, only a willingness to embrace whatever the journey brings. Be willing to adjust as the season informs existing goals. Don't fret about failure; it defines the contours of the next success.

Here is a non-exclusive list of goals to consider, suggestions to stoke the fires of your ambition:

1. Creation of an effective academic performance monitoring system
2. Developing effective relationships with referees
3. Improving mentoring skills
4. Winning the league title
5. Working effectively with each player
6. Teaching certain skills successfully
7. Having positive relationships with parents
8. Registering a winning record
9. Becoming a more effective listener
10. Making game adjustments that impact outcome

11. Earning the respect of other league coaches
12. Avoiding technicals
13. Doing an excellent job with teaching moments in practice
14. Learning how to trust players in game situations
15. Delegating effectively to assistants
16. Qualifying for postseason play
17. Filling the seats at home games
18. Inspiring the team to adopt the values of the program as their own
19. Becoming a better teacher of the game
20. Becoming a better game manager
21. These can be easily tweaked and supplemented. Your list is, well, *your* list. Be introspective. Reduce the list to writing. Don't overload yourself. Be selective and realistic. Whether you disclose any or all of your goals to the players is a judgment call. Sharing (to some extent) goals with players underscores the importance of setting goals, sets an example, and brings you closer to your players. If inclined to share, be careful not to overwhelm them with information that can confuse them or complicate your job, or, frankly, you deem too personal. Some goals are susceptible to disclosure; others may not be. It depends on your sensibilities and knowledge of your players, including their maturity levels.

Player Goals

Ask each player to write down their perceived strengths and weaknesses as basketball players. The list can include more than basic skills; it can also include intangibles (e.g., overcoming a short-fuse or low threshold of frustration in games or developing leadership skills). Once they complete the strengths and weaknesses list, meet with each player privately to develop specific achievable goals. Try to include your coaching staff in these sessions.

Goals can be short-term (e.g., shooting 50 foul shots a day outside of practice), long-term (e.g., improving an assist to turnover ratio), and phased (e.g., through use of specific cumulative goal deadlines). Make sure the goals are not grandiose but are articulated in small and incremental steps, which provide greater opportunity for success and reward. Once the initial goal-setting process is complete, players should reduce the results to writing and post them at home or in their team locker as constant reminders.

Team Goals

Developing a full slate of short- and long-term team goals can be challenging, if for no other reason than it requires achieving consensus among twelve or so high school players. Still, the process alone has intrinsic value. And, more than likely, the team will end up with a list each player supports. Keep in mind that your role is to facilitate the discussion, not dominate it or heavily influence the outcome. The team has to own the results, which cannot be top down.

Follow-up Meetings

Periodic review of work toward goals during the season is essential. The benefits of the goal-setting exercise are realized through a system that reviews progress, re-evaluates initial goals, makes appropriate changes, and, not the least, celebrates accomplishments—no matter how small or interim.

Further, player meetings not only allow a review of goals, they are also a forum to discuss other issues players might have, and, in the process, foster a deeper understanding of each player. They also advance the cherished value of communication, elevate the mission of the team over individual agenda, establish an atmosphere of inclusion, and generate respect and trust.

The Expectation Gap

As the season launches, coaches normally have a general sense of what their teams can reasonably accomplish, however measured. The difference between the starting and projected ending points a coach foresees for the team creates what I call an "expectation gap." Call it anticipated growth if you will. The overarching challenge is to grow progressively so the gap narrows and hopefully closes (or is transcended) as the season comes to a conclusion.

Often, however, our expectations reflect our *hopes* for the team, the ideal we envision or dream about. Passionate as we coaches can be, we are prone to romanticize the coaching experience and project more than what our team can produce. We sometimes get locked into how we believe players *should* perform and lose sight of what we realistically can expect of them.

When that happens, our hopes spawn expectations that outpace what players can produce, creating a "false expectation gap."

Realistic expectations can be a moving target over the course of the season, as initial projections can change with seasonal tides. Injuries, illnesses, and, perish the thought, suspensions can have major impacts on prospects and compel coaches to redefine expectations. More difficult, however, is getting a handle on how the actual capabilities of our athletes give rise to realistic expectations. There are substantial risks in expecting too much.

First, on a personal level, the more you unrealistically expect from your athletes, the greater the prospects for frustration for everyone, especially you. Coaching frustration is part and parcel of the coaching experience. It cannot be avoided. But it can be controlled and minimized. One way is to formulate realistic expectations for your team and individual players.

Importantly, try to identify when frustration is the product of your own disappointment rather than avoidable player failings like inattentiveness or lack of effort. We coaches are legendary for allowing our disappointments control how we communicate and perform as coaches. We need to work hard, internally, to own frustration triggered by unrealistic expectations or lack of patience.

Second, if you expect too much from players, and they know what you expect, as they typically do, you might set them up for failure. This is not to say you shouldn't push them to potential. You should. Nor is it to say your standards should not be high. They should be. It is, however, to say you should be clear on what is within their reach *and* grasp during the journey, an assessment that can change along the way. Small steps over time lead to big results.

Third, realistic expectations can effectively impact game adjustments and help you determine what your team needs to succeed in particular circumstances. For example, your team might have a history of allowing leads to evaporate down the stretch of games. No matter how well they have played while building leads, realistic expectations are what produce effective adjustments and strategies. They may need more help and guidance than they are willing to acknowledge and you may be instinctively inclined to give them. Strategy must account for probabilities and realistic expectations.

As the season evolves, coaches can benefit from a re-evaluation of early expectations. Reassessing—and often adjusting—expectations improves coaching effectiveness (and, as noted, reduces coaching frustration). Standing pat, in contrast, often means having expectations beyond what teams can deliver. Knowing your team well and being honest about what they can and cannot do will help the team navigate the challenges of a particular season and produce a sense of accomplishment that might otherwise escape them.

Communication

The art of effective communication, a lifelong pursuit, is front and center for the high school head coach. Effective communication—in the player-coach relationship (among several others)—means more than merely conversing and sharing words. To be effective, communication must be nuanced, contemplative, and meaningful. Here are brief and hopefully helpful thoughts in the context of the player-coach relationship (most of which apply to all relationships).

First, know your audience. While easier said than done, effective communication requires adapting your style and tone to the person with whom you are talking. What works with one player may not work with another, and vice versa. Strive to figure out what approach will allow you to reach and motivate each player.

Second, show genuine interest in your players. Affirm them with sincere questions. This will tend to make them more comfortable talking about themselves and feel heard, validated, and ultimately more trusting and receptive to what you have to say.

Third, be an active listener. *Hear* what they say, and even repeat what you heard to acknowledge you understand their perspective. You may not agree with or relate to all that is said, but you will begin to see things from their point of view.

Fourth, don't be defensive. As a coach, criticism is a way of life. Try not to take it personally. In addition, if you want to provide your perspective, do so without being argumentative. Using "I" rather "you" keeps the focus on your point of view and minimizes the risk that players will feel attacked or judged.

Fifth, maintain poise, not always easy when crazy stuff happens. When tested emotionally, stay cool. This will help keep the situation controlled, minimize relationship damage, and allow more productive dialogue.

Sixth, be inquisitive about the broader world of the player and try to understand the whole person. As a coach, especially if you are "off-campus" or a "walk-on," unless you make the effort, what you know about your athletes is a small slice of a large and complex pie. There is much more there than meets the eye, particularly during those often-bewildering teenage years.

Seventh, where applicable, understand the core emotions percolating in given circumstances. That, too, is no easy feat. You might instinctively be put off by the typical one- or two-word age-appropriate answers high schoolers offer. Find a way to dig deeper to build trust. It may take time, as players can be reticent and have limited attention span. But always remember: despite the youthful bravado and tough exterior, the heart of a child beats inside.

Eighth, be affirming. Your players deserve and—even though they will rarely, if ever, disclose it—crave your approval and positive acknowledgment, as persons and athletes. In the gym, praise loudly; criticize quietly.

Ninth, be firm but compassionate. You can be a good listener without being defensive and still hold your ground whenever you feel it necessary; you can be caring and resolute at once. The challenge is *how* you do it. This does not mean you shouldn't yield or compromise. Rather, it underscores that process and tone count for a lot.

Tenth, and finally, appreciate that player memories can fade or be selective. If practical and appropriate, have an assistant coach join you for at least the difficult meetings. And, don't be shy about confirming important understandings in writing.

Team Captains

L ike team parents, team captains should be se- lected at the earliest opportunity, ideally before the first preseason game. The process should not be too stressful, although it can have political overtones whenever a player craves captain status as a resume line item or a player has a sense of entitlement. Think expansively about how the captain selection process impacts the culture you are trying to nurture.

The Selection Process

Coaches and schools use different approaches to select team captains. Sometimes programs have an estab- lished custom and practice. ADs, for example, may re- quire or "suggest" a specific process. Most times, how- ever, you are free to determine. Regardless, know what preceded you and, in the case of an existing expectation in how to handle, confer with the AD to figure how best to proceed. This is another example where you are called upon to understand your institution.

Assuming you have a (relatively) free hand, here are some approaches.

First, you can have players vote for two or three captains, tally the votes, and announce the results. If you elect this approach, provide the team a list of qualities you believe captains should possess (see below). You can also require players to justify their choices with a few descriptive words. The process, as with every option, should be anonymous and confidential.

A disadvantage of this approach is that players sometimes select their friends, the best players, or popular players, or use other criteria inconsistent with what you advocate. Players don't always appreciate the minute qualities of leadership.

Second, alternatively, you can have the coaching staff select. A simple and straightforward approach, it allows you and your assistants to select captains you believe will acquit themselves well as *appointed* leaders of the team. Coaches are likely to select the most suitable candidates as captains and, because they control the selection process, are well-informed to address any backlash.

Third, you can combine the first two approaches, a combination of player input and coach discretion. Have the players *recommend* captains utilizing a process similar to the first approach, which the coaching staff can use to make final decisions. The twin virtues are that players have meaningful input and coaches the ultimate say. Again, the process should be anonymous and confidential.

In all cases, you can enhance the process by soliciting nominations, including self-nominations, and have nominated players address the team briefly (e.g., two minutes) to describe their commitment, motivations, and qualifications.

Captain Prototypes

Captain selection ideally should be informed by what is best for the team each year. Here are questions to frame the process:

1. Does the team need a forceful personality, someone who leads by example, or both?
2. Does the team need a skilled athlete whose accomplishments will inspire or a taskmaster who will keep the group moving and on message?
3. Is the team better off with single or multiple captains?
4. Do captains have to be seniors or can underclassmen fill the role?
5. Are there any politics to consider, including the prospect of an underclassman being selected over a senior or any players who feel entitled to get the nod?

Team Captain Selection Criteria

Each coach has their own vision of what comprises an effective captain. Reduce your list to writing and share it with the players so they can review and reflect on the characteristics you believe important. Here is a suggested list:

1. Mature
2. Role model in practices and games, and model program ambassador to the public
3. Commands the respect of teammates
4. First-rate representative of the team in games, especially when dealing with referees
5. Mentally tough
6. Coachable and receives criticism constructively
7. Team-first player with a great work ethic
8. Consistently reinforces team values
9. Consistently positive
10. Has leadership skills
11. Has healthy respect for the traditions of the program
12. Seeks challenges
13. Will support the decisions of the coaching staff, whether or not agrees with them
14. Can communicate effectively
15. Will treat teammates in practice and game situations with trust and respect
16. Understands that each player is an integral part of the whole

The Duties and Responsibilities of the Captain

Captains are an extension of the coaching staff and help shape the direction of the team. Once they are selected, lay out what you expect of them—effectively a job description. Typically, their responsibilities fall into three categories of duties: team ambassador and liaison, leader, and role model:

Team Ambassador and Liaison. Team captains serve as appointed representatives of the team. They are an essential interface between the team and coaches and should confer with the coaching staff whenever team concerns have arisen or begun to sprout. They are expected to shine brightly as ambassadors of the community whenever in public, especially during games, road trips, and team outings. They are charged with helping resolve various team or player conflicts, addressing any player backbiting, negativity, and complaining, and holding teammates accountable. In addition, they are expected to work respectfully with referees to improve the quality and fairness of competition and, whenever appropriate, advocate for the team.

Team Leaders. Team captains are expected to be supportive of teammates during practices and games, especially where they are struggling and need a lift. They should be quick to praise and encourage teammates and the team as a whole, in practices and games, especially in tough situations. They should have the backs of their teammates.

Role Models. Team captains should be the first to confront violations of team rules and set an example of behavior in accordance with what is expected of everyone on the team. They must consistently demonstrate sportsmanship in practices and in games in a manner that honors the values of the school. Importantly, they must strive to be consistent in words and actions.

Leadership Beyond Captains

Leadership in team sports is critical and everyone, whether appointed captain or not, who can and is willing to lead should be encouraged to do so. The team needs to know that team leaders are not limited to appointed captains and that leadership comes from within and can be expressed in many ways. While only captains should handle certain roles (as discussed earlier), others should be free and encouraged to lead in a manner comfortable to them. Coaches should be attentive to detect *emergent* leaders—who often command instant respect from teammates—and encourage them to lead within their personalities and comfort zones.

The Care and Feeding of Your Athletic Director

Your AD relationship is vitally important. Fundamentally, the AD is your immediate supervisor—your boss—a reality coaches can sometimes forget since, in their day-to-day world, they enjoy significant leeway in how they do their jobs, much of which escapes AD scrutiny. That is the nature of the job, but it also means it is easy to succumb to the allure of seeming independence. As a result, it is helpful to have an internal check as a reminder of the chain of command and your accountability. It is even more important to make a thriving, positive, and mutually rewarding AD relationship a high priority and an indispensable part of how you function as a coach. It begins with understanding how your program fits within the larger context of the AD world.

The Vision and Expectations of the AD

Each AD has a vision for the athletic program they oversee and the culture they want to build and sustain. Each coach at the school, in turn, has a role to play to help realize the AD's vision through the building of a specific sports program. This does not mean each program cannot and should not have its own identity, only that the contours of each sports program are but a piece of a larger puzzle. Thus, know what the AD deems important and expects of you within the overall landscape of the school athletic program. Here is a general picture from the AD perspective.

Value-Based Program Building. Fundamentally, your AD wants you to build a vibrant program community that advances the values of the school. This generally translates to a "journey"-based, not an "end results"-based, program. ADs tend to see coaches more as "teachers" of high school students before they are "coaches" of athletes. To them, wins and losses and the traditional measures of success, while holding value, are less important than players learning life tools for success, how to become model citizens, and how to win with honor, demonstrating sportsmanship consistently and taking pride in everything they do, among similar values. Seek to unlock the collective power of your athletes within the scope of what the school is trying to accomplish.

ADs want their coaches to inspire athletes to play for the joy and love of the game, not to please the coaching staff. Teach players that "love" in an athletic program can be expressed in various ways, by, for example, supporting a teammate who has missed a shot or committed an error, taking a stand against behavior detrimental to the team, or showing respect for each teammate.

Positive Relationships and Effective Communication. Most ADs will tell you the key to head coaching success is effective and motivating communication and the most successful coaches are the best communicators. Positive reinforcement works; negative commentary does not. Candor and transparency are equally important. Be upfront with the athletes and don't surprise them about what they can expect. And, don't feel you need to have an answer to every question from a player, parent, or member of the community. Better to circle back after some homework than risk misspeaking.

Thriving Learning Environment. From the vantage point of the AD, it is all about the kids. ADs want to see a positive environment where athletes can thrive, have fun, and are thrilled to be there. They want coaches to find the gift in each student-athlete, build their confidence, and make each feel special. Kids arrive with different life experiences, backgrounds, motivations, and skill sets. ADs want their coaches to find a way to get them all on the same page and help them become better persons within the parameters of who they are.

Leadership. ADs are mindful, and appreciate, that coaches spend more time with student-athletes than everyone else at the school and sometimes even more than parents. Successful coaches are good role models who fully appreciate the influence they have on the kids and understand they are *always* "on" and watched, no matter the moment. Effective coaches don't try to befriend their players, but rather try to be another adult in their lives who works to help them identify themselves, honor boundaries, navigate life challenges, and balance and distinguish what is important in the moment versus what is important for the future. It is often less important what happens the next ten minutes than ten years from now.

Accountability. The school holds students accountable in all they do as students. The same should apply to your athletes. Your baseline is consistency. Be clear about what you expect and be consistent with your style. Don't be a rollercoaster, up one day and down the next. You will have your bad days, but strive for consistency in everything you do. Be realistic, however, about what they can do. Form sensible expectations.

Accountability applies to you as well. Always be prepared to defend your decisions in whatever context—game or otherwise—you make them. Address problems as they arise. Delay tends to compound problems.

Performance. Be a student of your sport and open to change. Know the sport well and never stop learning. Be detailed oriented. Don't fear mistakes. The same goes for your athletes. Teach them that high school athletics provides unique opportunities to fall down one day and get up and come back the next.

The Real World of the AD

An awareness of what your AD faces day to day, as well as overall, will improve how you work with the AD.

The job of the modern high school AD almost defies description. They have become, in essence, universal problem-solvers, consistently pulled in multiple directions. For example, parents are more involved than ever in the athletic endeavors of their children; indeed, many argue far too involved. Unlike a time gone by, today if a parent is unhappy with the athlete experience of their child, their instinct is to make a beeline for the AD's office, notwithstanding school protocol that specifies the coach as the first line of communication. ADs also have to monitor student-athlete grades and help devise ways to support those who struggle. They often have to deal with student-athlete discipline, which can be difficult and sometimes include law enforcement. They have to implement athletic budgets that teeter under the weight of all sports programs vying for limited funds and in the process assure fairness. They have to resolve competition for facility usage, especially during the basketball season when multiple teams may need more gym access than circumstances allow. They have to help with certain travel, get officials for home games, work with booster groups to generate additional funds for their athletic programs, set up gyms for home games, buy equipment and athletic apparel, hire coaches, and on and on. And, lest we forget, ADs must process endless amounts of paperwork. Appreciate, too, that at most high schools, ADs are instrumental in preserving and implementing school culture. High school sports are pervasively visible in the community and, in consequence, the athletic program serves as school marketer and ambassador to the world. This means that ADs must carefully monitor how scores of teams in multiple sports represent the school and assure each team advances school values.

Does this mean you should be a shrinking violet in dealing with your AD and not advocate for what you want? Definitely not! The point is, as you move forward in implementing your program, keep the huge expanse of what the AD faces constantly in mind, so you can wisely and prudently use the AD relationship to advance the goals of your program.

Individual Working Relationship

Not surprisingly, ADs have different working styles. They range from micro-management to hands-off. If you don't know the style of yours out of the box, you will find out soon enough. Whatever it is, know it well and adjust accordingly. The extremes of micro-management and hands-off each come with their problems; the former can stifle and the latter can want for sufficient support. Figure out how best to use whatever style lies in front of you to program advantage. And remember, even if your AD is hands-off, it does not mean they don't want visits from you or to be kept informed. They do!

Build a collaborative AD relationship through regular, clear, and open communication. You may not always agree or share the same vision, but you can learn from each other.

Your AD can be your champion and, often, your confidant. Develop trust and don't be shy about consulting the AD on matters of concern. Your AD wants you to succeed.

Know when, what and how the AD wants information. An informed AD is a happy AD. Similarly, be sensitive to issues you know or reasonably suspect the AD would want to hear about. *Anticipate* those issues. Be careful, very careful, not to spring surprises on your AD or, worse, have others do so. The "blindside" is one of the worst things that can happen to your AD relationship. On the other hand, unless instructed otherwise, handle the petty stuff yourself. Don't bother the AD with each little item that arises unless you genuinely need help, although when in doubt, consult.

Understand and honor the chain of command. Never go over the head of your AD. Know the policies and rules of the athletic department. Know what your AD expects of you as a coach like the back of your hand. Know what bugs and what thrills them.

Be reliable and responsive. In this regard, handle your paperwork responsibilities like a tax return. ADs are swamped with paperwork and don't need to take on yours as well.

Finally, keep in mind ADs have good ideas and valuable program input. While in many instances they will not know hoops like you, they will know how to run high school athletic programs and are well-schooled in the nuances of player-coach and parent-coach relationships. While you should constantly strive to propose your own solutions to problems, ADs can be invaluable in assisting with problem-solving.

Your working relationship will develop over time. Like every relationship, there is the honeymoon phase, and then as the road traveled reveals course inversions, curves, and bumps, you will refine the relationship.

The Care and Feeding of Parents

As mentioned in Chapter 13, parents today are more involved in high school athletics than ever before, and sometimes to a degree many commentators, coaches, and athletic directors, not to mention some parents as well, find problematic. No matter where you coach you will experience parents thrusting themselves into your program, whether to complain about playing time or tell you how to coach, among other things. It is a fact of coaching life.

Be that as it may, to serve players well, head coaches must find ways to develop effective, meaningful, and positive relationships with parents. Consider these tools.

First, the most important tool is effective communication. The communication principles described in Chapter 11 apply with equal force here, and while they are not a guarantee of smooth waters, without them, you might become awash in a downpour of complaints and political turmoil. Be proactive. Establish a rapport with each parent, knowing that, as with all relationships, you will warm to some more than others. Seek out your AD to get a preview of what concerns at this school parents tend to have. Be prepared and anticipate.

Second, hold an early parent group meeting to set a positive tone for the season and discuss the program, rules, and expectations—and boundaries (e.g., no discussions about Xs and Os, how to run your practices, or playing time). The potluck described in Chapter 7 is the perfect opportunity. If for any reason you don't hold a kickoff potluck, organize an early parent meeting dedicated to the topics described in Chapter 7. Consider also creating a team handbook with the same information.

Third, when it comes to mentoring and guidance, a gray area overlaps the roles parents and coaches play for student-athletes. Both coaches and parents are involved in the ever-important task of teaching life lessons. Know that your influence has limits, which are basketball-program defined. This can be hard when events occur outside of school that directly impact your program and draw you into the mix, including wayward player behavior and family strife. There can be times, because of concern for a player, you feel compelled to venture deep into the gray area. Make sure you are welcome and be cautious. Don't hesitate to get guidance from your AD.

Fourth, keep a steady flow of information. Regular group communications through email or other effective means are important. Parents and players need reminders. They have much on their plates and may not be as attentive to, or organized around, basketball program details as you prefer. You can use text messages as a supplemental or speedy form of communication, but group information assures timely, effective, and clear communication. Consider, for example, providing parents and players a weekly email with the upcoming week's schedule as a reminder, even though you presented the entire schedule to them at the start of the season or it can found on the school website. Making their lives easier makes yours easier as well.

Fifth, as discussed in Chapter 13, keep your AD posted on all major parent issues and, where possible, anticipate them with your AD. Protect yourself.

Sixth, be accessible. Have a response time rule (e.g., always respond to a parent communication within 24 hours, if not substantively, at least to acknowledge them with a promised follow-up). Be willing to hold private meetings with parents, subject to school meeting protocols. Bring an assistant and memorialize the meeting in writing, either within the administration or directly with the parent whenever appropriate to confirm understandings. And, except in extreme situations where confidentiality is important, try not to meet with a parent without the player present.

Seventh, although you should be an active listener to whatever parents have to say, don't be reluctant to stand up for what you're trying to accomplish. Don't let pressure cower you. Be honest and as transparent as reasonably appropriate, but nonetheless firm. For example, although you will be asked, you cannot give your blessing to missed games or other team events due to family reasons. Respect their choice and decision, but they must understand that leaving the team for any discretionary reason bears consequences. Be keen to emphasize the critical interplay of choices, decisions, and consequences (CDC).

Eighth, don't assume parental motives, tempting as that may be. Deal with issues on the merits. And, keep in mind that most parents lack coaching experience and are narrowly focused on their child. For the most part, they are well-intentioned. Keep remembering they have entrusted their children to the school (and your program) and, in the end, want their children to succeed (however defined). Assume they are coming from a good place and try to get them to see the wider program picture and the greater good. Be a "perspective provider."

Ninth, advocate to parents the importance of positivity and support of the team, especially during games by respecting officials and opponents, and praising and not criticizing student-athletes. Create a standard worthy of emulation.

Tenth, in the extreme situation where a parent loses control and blows up, try to stay poised and don't get defensive. Do not interrupt, and do what you can to bring the tone down to a level of civility. Keep the focus on the player, not the parent or you. Stay positive; in other words, practice what you preach!

Finally, appreciate that despite adherence to these principles, and no matter how well-meaning you are and how much support your AD supplies, you may sometimes experience an incurably disgruntled parent. You will not satisfy everyone. Respect the limits of your effectiveness and take comfort knowing you did your part to make it work.

The care and feeding of parents require patience, adherence to values, consultation with those you trust, and interpersonal tools you can refine through experience. You will make mistakes. But if you stay committed to what is important to you and the program, you will emerge a better coach and person.

Practices

You probably thought we would never arrive at the fun part of coaching: practices! For sure, practices are enormous fun—hard work yes, but fun. Practice is also where coaches place their unique signature on each season. The gym is the basketball coach's temple-sanctuary, where coaching thrives unimpeded by the outside world. It is the largest, most energy-infused classroom on campus, where we guide, teach, provoke, and exhort and give expression to our passion-driven vision and where everyone is expected to leave the outside world at the door.

Motivated coaches champ at the bit to get into gym each day to blow the whistle, gather the players, and get to work. Each coach plans and runs practices their own way. In devising yours, gather information. Observe the practices of other coaches, at all levels if possible. Read materials, watch videos, and attend clinics. There is a literal compendium of helpful information out there. Be studious and get inspired.

Here is a general lay of the land.

Practice Organization

Planning Frequency. Decide whether to plan one day at a time or prepare a few days or more in advance. A conservative approach to start is moving in small steps and playing things by ear until you reach your comfort level. One effective approach is to plan each week based on what you want to accomplish that week and then tweak the plan each day to reflect how it is playing out as you move through the week and toward weekly goals. However you proceed, reduce each practice plan to writing. That allows you to plan and organize better and cover what you want efficiently. Share copies with assistants timely so they know what to expect in advance each day. Confer with them each day about what to do the next. Also, consider posting your practice sheet in the gym before practice so players can see what awaits them that day. Perhaps include a thought or quote of the day.

Time Allocation. Allocate each minute of the entire practice to an activity, including team meetings and hydration breaks, knowing you may occasionally diverge from the script (e.g., for a drill that needs more time).

As a general guide, except for scrimmages or work on offensive systems, limit drills to four to eight minutes.

Alternating Drills. Consider alternating tougher and less "exciting" drills (e.g., certain defensive drills) with more "enjoyable" drills (e.g., shooting or ballhandling). You can lose your audience if you stack too many tough drills in succession. Further, certain drills are better in the first half of practice than the second and vice versa, (e.g., an intrasquad scrimmage or 5-on-5 half court offense tends to be better suited for later in practice.

Activity Emphasis. While your coaching philosophy is your starting point, what you emphasize in practice should reflect what you believe the team needs to succeed. This can change over the course of the season as game performance reveals particular weak spots or vital areas needing improvement (e.g., rebounding or foul shooting). To keep yourself honest, tally the percentages of time you devote to all activities (offense, defense, conditioning, special situations, foul shooting, rebounding, and so on) to see whether they match the emphasis you and your staff believe are necessary for team success. Be aware of spending time on activities you may long to do but are not what the team needs.

Similarly, it is not unusual to change practice focus deep into the season. What you generally stress during the early part of the season may not be what is needed in the latter part. For example, legs tire as the end of the season nears. In consideration, you might shift away from conditioning and transition drills. You might even shorten practices (e.g., from 120 to 90 minutes). At some point, the overriding practice purpose is getting teams specific game-ready and an extra 20-30 minutes may produce diminishing returns.

The Tone of Practice

In deciding what specifically to run in practice, first consider what kind of tone and energy you want in the gym at the onset of practice. The following questions can help shape your practice atmosphere each day.

1. When do you want players to arrive for practice relative to the start time? Is being on time *late* or is being early (e.g., 15 minutes) *on time?*

2. Do you want your players to hit the ground running at the start time, meaning fully stretched and focused before the start whistle blows, or do you prefer to allocate warm-up time to the start of practice?

3. If an option, should you run time off the game scoreboard down to the start time of practice to get players initially focused and clock conscious?

4. On the whistle or buzzer to start practice, do you expect players sharply to stop whatever they are doing, get silent, and sprint to where the team is expected to assemble?

5. Regarding practice decorum, do your players understand that a tweet of the whistle triggers

complete silence, and if you then speak, ALL eyes are on you?

6. Do you start practice with a team cheer? What are the last words or sounds you want the team to hear before practice work begins?

Develop routines to shape the gym. What you select should be designed to incite spirit, establish a discipline standard and create practice decorum.

Practice Content

Opening Meeting. Before the start of practice, convene a brief meeting to review what is planned for practice, any relevant seasonal developments, and where the team stands in the overall journey. Challenge each player to be better when practice is over than when it started. Challenge them to ask how they can be a better teammate in the upcoming practice. Break for practice with energy.

The Degree of Practice Difficulty. Practice should be hard. You are preparing them for game competition. Practice should be more difficult than what games require of them. Set the practice bar high. Get feedback from the team or at least its leadership about whether practices are testing the team enough. Have them endorse the challenge.

Fundamentals. It is hard to spend too much time on basketball fundamentals, at least early in the season. There are many to consider, including ball handling,

the jump stop, rebounding techniques, shooting me-
chanics, defensive footwork and stances, pass fakes,
shot fakes, post entry passes, catching the ball in the
post, help defense, use of hands on defense, team communication, and so on. However your practices evolve
during the year, fundamentals—and the little things—
never lose their essential importance.

Drills. Each drill should have a purpose, if not multiple purposes, and represent the essential vehicle by
which the team can succeed. Monitor which drills are
working and which are not, not only from a skill development perspective, but also in terms of engagement
and player attention to detail. And while in the main
drills should vigorously push players toward individual
and team goals, every now and then insert a drill for
pure fun sake.

Also, select drills that minimize the amount of time
players stand around. Spots of idleness cannot be to-
tally avoided, but the less time players stand around, the
more time they are engaged and enjoy the experience.

Competitive Drills. Players are motivated by activities
they can win. Competition tends to bring out their best
effort and, for that reason, practice drills should include tailored competitive consequences.

In this regard, a successful coaching tool is to select teams for each practice and score various drills
throughout practice, using cumulative scoring, drill by
drill. While it is not practical to score all practice drills,

you can be creative by using non-traditional scoring. For example, if you run the defensive shell drill, you can specify that the only way to register points is on defense (e.g., 3 points for a charge, 2 points for all other turnovers and 1 point for a defensive stop. The next drill (e.g., a shooting drill) can emphasize mid-range shots off the dribble, with traditional scoring that adds to the cumulative numbers.

You can follow the drills part of practice with a half court scrimmage, with each team starting with the cumulative points amassed over the course of practice. When the half court scrimmage arrives at the end of practice, teams have a total cumulative score that stays on the scoreboard to start the scrimmage. The scrimmage continues the cumulative scoring. You can end the competition with a foul shooting drill, which can inspire the team that is behind to finish the scrimmage strong in the hope of winning the day's competition by taking advantage of the foul shooting final phase.

If you assemble competitive teams for the entirety of practice, you have to decide whether to balance the teams or pit starters against non-starters. Some coaches favor the hierarchy. Others prefer to balance. Some use a balance but transition to a hierarchal approach for specific game preparation. Consider team morale and specifically how the non-starters will react if routinely pitted against the starters, as well as what approach will produce the maximum player improvement and get players game-ready.

The Gym Din. What do your practices *sound* like? To what extent do your players communicate during practice in team-building ways? Test them. Close your eyes during practice for short periods. What do you hear? Does it meet your expectations? Talk to them about this. It is important. Never forget: a noisy gym reveals a team with an edge and presumed game advantage. Get your players to talk it up, constantly. The less they hear your voice (except to teach, encourage, and affirm) and the more they hear the voices of each other, the more powerful they will be as a unit.

The Scoreboard Clock. Presumably you will time your drills, either with a hand-held stopwatch mechanism or the game scoreboard. Using the scoreboard, for all to see, helps players become more clock conscious, which can help in games.

Building Habits. A major practice goal is to build good habits, the glue of effective game performance. Habits generate sound instincts. This can happen only with repetition in practice. If you want your players, for example, to have great defensive footwork, drill footwork all the time. By way of another example, you cannot expect your players to take charges in games, which requires some chutzpah, unless you have regular charging drills in practice. This does not mean using the same drills each day—you should mix them up—but regular drills that refine the particular skills you hold important.

Practice Scrimmages. It is important to have full court intra-squad scrimmages from time to time. It is generally better to hold them during practice on Saturdays or at least not before a game day since they require more energy, although you might find that some teams thrive on a robust scrimmage the night before a game. Half court scrimmages also are extremely helpful and can be used daily, especially to work on offensive and defensive systems. In either case, you can impose certain rules and conditions that emphasize certain aspects of your systems. You can also run situational drills using the half court and full court scrimmage format. See next section.

Situational Drills. Coaches spend the vast majority of practice time on fundamentals, conditioning, skill development, offensive and defensive systems, and scrimmages, and then complain they don't have enough time even for those activities. Finding practice time, on top of everything else, for anticipated game situations is challenging. But remember that practice is geared toward game preparation, a dress rehearsal for the real stage. Why not *regularly* allocate practice time to specific game situations?

Players need a comfort level to feel adept at handling game situations before they face them. Their confidence in pressure situations is stronger when they have seen them in practice, especially if the rigor in practice matches or exceeds game intensity. Expecting players to handle special game situations effectively without practicing them is not realistic. Players simply perform better in familiar situations.

The subject of situational basketball is covered fully in my book *Odds-On Basketball Coaching: Crafting High-Percentage Strategies in Game Situations* (https://tinyurl. com/y7xwz6vd).

Stations. Stations are an effective and efficient way to isolate drills based on player roles (e.g., guards and bigs). The same is true for conditioning stations that have players rotate to spots for conditioning activity (e.g., jump rope, planks, agility ladder work, dribbling in place, pushups, sit ups, back board touches, and so on).

Conditioning. Ideally, players should arrive at tryouts in top shape. That, however, is more exception than rule, and coaches must spend considerable practice time on conditioning. Many drills combine skill work with conditioning, allowing you to accomplish multiple goals with one drill. On occasion, you may want to run outright conditioning drills, especially the first weeks of the season. If you do, make sure the conditioning work is specifically tailored to basketball conditioning (e.g., short bursts of speed, changes of speed, jumping ability, specialized weight room work, and so on).

Film Sessions. Film is a powerful teaching tool. It is also a reality check. Watching film of your games with players is illuminating to say the least. Further, if you have the resources, and the time, create film splices of individual game performance. Players are often astonished what they learn about themselves from watching film. The film doesn't lie!

Be aware about diminishing attention in the film room. At some point in group sessions, and much earlier than you would like, your players will fidget and lose focus. Know your team's attention span and plan accordingly.

Watching film of upcoming opponents is similarly helpful. Again, if you have the resources, have them watch opponent game film on their own. Certain software programs allow you to monitor when each player logs on and off the film site and allows the coaching staff to keep abreast of who is spending the time and who is not.

Teaching Moments. Be ever mindful of teaching moments in practice. While you do not want to blow your whistle every 10 seconds, identify appropriate moments to illustrate a teaching point, especially to commend a player for something done well for all to emulate. When you do stop practice to teach, don't linger. Attention spans are limited. Make your point succinctly—even have a personal "seven second" rule (or something similar)—and resume practice to minimize disruption to practice flow.

Teaching moments become more frequent when working on offensive and defensive systems. It is important to simplify systems, through teaching and breakdown drills, to make sure players are clear on the concepts. In these circumstances, you likely will need to spend more time talking at the front end of the learning process to walk them through and review the intricacies of systems and plays.

Maybe the biggest challenge in practices is extricating players from bad habits, which, generally, should be addressed as they surface (either publicly or privately as appropriate). Sometimes, however, you may have to pick your spots. You cannot cure everything right away. Gauge each player's willingness and ability to change so you can effectively guide them without overloading them.

Assistants and Player Support. Have assistants craft and run drills in practice. Keep ideas flowing and give players another voice to hear. The same is true with players. Be bold and have a player run a practice or some drills. Again, another voice and perspective can be an effective teaching tool.

Getting Ready for First Game. Be mindful of the date of your first game. While you might place less emphasis on offensive systems than on fundamentals and conditioning in early practices, you will need minimal game preparation in place for the first few games, including man and zone half court offense, in-bounds

plays, sideline out of bounds plays, press offense, a half
court defensive system, ball screens and pick and roll
defense, and whatever else you feel they need before
the first jump ball of the season. As a general guide,
install your main offensive system within three weeks.

Ending Practice. Try to end each practice on an up-
beat note, and, as much as practical, have a consistent ending to practice. Assemble everyone at the end
for a brief meeting to review the practice. Stress what
they did well and focus them on the next challenge. Be
positive and encouraging. Make them feel good about
themselves, even if they struggled. If they had lapses,
don't ignore them, but encourage them to address any
issues the next practice. Make them feel you care and
are committed to them. End with a team cheer.

Brief Thoughts on a Defensive System

Successful defense features discipline, intensity, energy, effort, and desire, each of which players control. Defense is the common denominator skill set. It is the fastest way to be competitive. A team able to get stops with relative consistency is always in the game, even if the ball is not dropping with regularity at the other end. Similarly, defensive rebounds trigger transition and secondary offense opportunities, which can fill gaps from a bad shooting night or lackluster half court offense. And, not the least, a ferocious defense can deflate the spirit of the other team and build game momentum. Defense breeds game success.

Whatever defensive systems and tactics you use will flow from a blend of your personnel, philosophy, passion, leadership and, yes, personality. Every team has an identity. For some it is a brand of offense (e.g., a heavy emphasis on a three-point shooting attack) and for others it might be a style of defense (e.g., aggressive half court trapping). Regardless of the specific identify you forge for your team, make defense a priority in your overall system.

Know Your Personnel (KYP)

A bedrock coaching principle is: know your personnel. As is often said: "It is not about the Xs and the Os; it's about the Jimmies and the Joes." Effective systems depend on their relevance to specific players. A fast team can run; a slow team cannot. Teams quick on their feet are more suited to press than slower-footed teams. Philosophy matters little if your players lack the skills and physicality to execute what you, from 30,000 feet, are prone to advocate. It is beautiful to see coaches with an abiding passion for playing the game a certain way, but be sure what you love to do is what your players can do.

Skill Development

Leaving technique for another day, here is an illustrative list of specific defensive skills you might develop during your program, some of which can be practiced within the same drill:

1. *Footwork and Stance.* Defensive footwork, including stance, is the essence of effective individual defense. Repetitive practice of the push, step and slide, and proper stance should be a mainstay of your practices.

2. *Use of the Hands.* Coaches differ in the placement (and movement) of hands on defense for example, some like players to spread their arms like wings and control the space, others like a hand near the ball (in the shot pocket) and the other arm out looking to deflect a pass or stymie a dribble drive. Decide what is most effective for your defensive style.

3. *On-the-Ball Defense.* The cousin of defensive footwork and effective use of the hands, on-the-ball defensive skills require consistent drills.

4. *Controlling a Dribbler.* In the half court, players should be able to contain a dribbler for a least three dribbles.

5. *Denying Dribble Penetration.* Part of playing on-the-ball defense is being able to adapt to different players with the ball. Do they favor one side of the floor or one hand? Do they have a quick first step and command some separation to control their direction? Work consistently on keeping opponents out of the paint.

6. *Shading Baseline.* On-the-ball defense also includes the ability to push ballhandlers away from

the middle of the court and toward the baseline, and, in the process, disrupt the offense, reduce chances of a good shot, and increase baseline help and trapping options.

7. *Closing Out Shooters.* This is a skill that has escaped most high school players, as it has virtually the entire NBA. Today, players are enamored of the prospects of blocking the perimeter shot, a hero moment that happens with unsurprising infrequency. The goal of the closeout is three-fold, none of which includes shot blocking: (a) lower the percentage chance of any take, (b) get in good position for any upfake and attempted dribble-drive, and (c) take away the shot and bottle up the shooter. Long live the stutter-step.

8. *Staying Down.* Players too often take the bait of an upfake and yield control, which often sends the offensive player to the foul line. Drill relentlessly into your players that staying down on potential shooters is a badge of defensive honor.

9. *Taking Charges.* Players seldom seek charges for a simple reason: coaches don't practice the technique enough. Taking a charge is no day at the beach. It is a specific skill and requires familiarity. And, yes, it requires toughness, which might come naturally for some players, but for others requires *repetition in practice.* The charge takes away a possession, can change momentum or at

least provide a lift, and adds to the foul count of the other team.

10. *Ball Denial.* Learning to deny a pass, whether specific to a possession, part of a game strategy to keep the ball out of the hands of a dominant scorer or playmaker or integral to how you play defense generally, is a skill integral to effective defense.

11. *The Deflection.* This is maybe the most neglected defensive skill. I once saw a team completely disrupt the offense of an opponent for an entire half with constant deflections, forcing the offense out of planned sets and causing many turnovers. Value (and record) deflections.

12. *Trapping.* Players struggle sometimes to trap smartly, mostly because they want to get their hands on the ball. They must learn to embrace the limits of the role of the trapper, which is to mirror the ball, maintain the trap, obstruct passing lanes, and possibly get a deflection. Any steal is left to teammates hunting passing lines. If trapping is integral to your defense, repetitive drills to hone trapping techniques will pay huge dividends.

13. *Dead Ball Defense.* The loss of an offensive player's dribble is an opportunity to execute a "solo" trap to smother the player and force a bad pass or a five-second call. It also means the rest of

team should *deny the ball* to the players they are guarding.

14. *Boxing Out.* You cannot do enough box-out drills.

15. *"The "Wall."* When guarding in the low post area, players have a tendency to reach, wave, and bump. Better they learn to crowd their player chest to chest, move in parallel with the opponent, and keep arms straight up in the air, like a full body mirror. The Wall can make things awkward for the other player and reduce the percentage chance of any take without fouling.

Team Defense: Man

Every high school team plays man defense, and some more than others. Start with a threshold reality: teams will score against your man defense regardless. A man defense predicated on stops each possession misses the mark. Instead, focus on probabilities and specific achievable goals (e.g., forcing the ball away from high percentage scorers, limiting second chance opportunities, minimizing paint penetration, getting back with urgency in transition defense, employing defensive techniques that lower the percentage chances of shots, and forcing the offense to do things they don't want to do and making them spend a lot of time doing them).

The components of a man defensive system are common to most programs but what you emphasize depends on your style and philosophy. Consider the following.

1. *The Intangibles.* Preach defensive intangibles constantly—determination, discipline, trust, communication, commitment, and pride.

2. *Help Defense, Including Helping the Helper and Player Rotations.* Needless to say, teaching teams how to rotate to implement help defense, including helping the initial helper, is critical to the success of team defense. The two biggest challenges teams face at the high school level is learning to anticipate movement to help and trusting that someone will help them after they help another. Players need extensive work seeing the ball and keeping an eye on whom they are guarding. They must learn that man defense is much more than guarding an assigned player. It is a buddy system. They must learn when to leave their player by anticipating penetration and when to recover, if practical, to their original assignment. Repetitive work in practice, like with the shell drill, will help increase trust and anticipation.

3. *Strongside Defense.* Strongside defense is about spacing and positioning (and of course communication). You have to decide whether you prefer to deny the ball one pass away or have your off-the-ball defenders on the strongside "up and on the line" to help on penetration. What you do

might be a function of game strategy or a general approach that fits your athletes best.

4. *Weak Side Defense.* Weak side defense is based on positioning and movement with the ball. Players should be taught that, when on the weak side, to stay between the player they are guarding and the ball (and constantly see both), while at the same time be close enough to the player being guarded to stop any penetration or execute a close out on ball reversal or skip pass, and also close enough to help, if appropriate, on dribble penetration.

5. *Transition Defense and Defensive Balance.* How you handle defensive balance against transition is a game-by-game judgment. But your team should be schooled in how to protect against transition offense, whether keeping one or two guards back, contesting the outlet pass, matching up with the outlet receiver, or combinations.

6. *Low Post Defense.* The essential strategies are fronting the post, playing behind the post, or using a three-quarter front that seeks to deny the pass. The chosen strategy most of the time will be game-specific depending on matchups. You should also be prepared to double-team the post in certain situations.

7. *Defending Post Cuts.* Players, particularly wing and perimeter defenders, should be schooled in how to handle cuts to the basket after post entry.

8. *Defending Backdoor Cuts.* The same is true for the backdoor cut. There is little more frustrating than a player getting beat by a backdoor cut.

Team Defense: Zone

For coaches who do not hate zone defenses—and frankly for those who do—have at least one zone defense in your playbook. Whether a traditional zone—like a 2-3, a matchup zone, or both—the time will come when trotting out a zone for parts (or all) of a game will be in the best interest of your team. Executed well, zones are not soft. They are (or should be) aggressive and unsettling to the other side. They have several advantages.

1. They slow down offenses. If a slower pace in a particular circumstance favors you, a zone can control tempo.

2. Zones can minimize or eliminate matchup disadvantages that may exist in man defense.

3. The zone is particularly effective against a poor passing team. Zone offense, to be successful, must move the ball, and with it, defenders. The more passes a poor passing team makes, the greater chances of a miscue.

4. The zone can protect a player in foul trouble, by allowing you to more easily "hide" that player, which is especially attractive when the player is important to the offense.

5. Zones (especially matchup zones) are effective against weak perimeter shooting teams that rely heavily on dribble penetration.

6. Strategically, zone defense can complement man defense. Tossing a zone at an opponent, particularly following a long stretch of man defense, can confuse the other team. Also, alternating defenses off your offense (e.g., zone on a make and man on a miss) can stymie the other team and deny them offensive rhythm.

7. A matchup zone, aggressively executed, can drive offenses to distraction. Using zone spacing and man-to-man defensive principles, they are effective in preventing dribble penetration and impairing ball movement, making perimeter shooting more difficult.

8. If the zone is your main defense, you may want to reallocate substantial practice time otherwise reserved for man defensive work.

You should be able to find a place in your defensive arsenal to create advantage from zone defenses.

Defensive Communication

Here is a truism: teams that communicate effectively on defense are more successful than teams that don't. Yet, getting players to talk on defense—a skill displayed with gusto outside the gym—is sometimes no mean feat. It is something coaches have to remind players to do constantly, even nag them about, and even have specific consequences in practice in competitive team drills commensurate with the quality of team communication. It is that important. It breeds cohesion, improves play, and intimidates opponents.

Communication should be evident in several circumstances of the game: (a) alerting teammates to an impending screen, (b) alerting the entire team to a launched shot, (c) announcing when guarding the ball, (d) announcing a skip pass, (e) informing teammates of a help position, (f) identifying who a player is guarding or moving to guard, (g) calling rebound, and (h) giving general teammate encouragement.

Good and Bad Fouls

Players should appreciate the differences between "good" fouls committed for advantage and "bad" fouls that harm team prospects. Create a list of both and make sure players know the differences. Have a meeting to discuss the list and even test them. Make each a part of the team lexicon. See *Odds-On Basketball Coaching: Crafting High-Percentage Strategies in Game Situations* (https://tinyurl.com/y7xwz6vd) for an in-depth discussion of good and bad fouls.

Pressure and Traps

No question, pressure defense—whether in the form of a full court, 3/4 court or half court press, or various traps—can be a powerful weapon. Before getting too excited about the prospects, however, make sure your team is well suited for what you have in mind. Do you have sufficient player depth with requisite skill sets for an uptempo and aggressive defense? Do you have players who can read passing lanes, anticipate passes, and, vitally, understand rotations in the larger court spacing? Do your athletes have sufficient quickness and agility? Are they sufficiently conditioned? If you like the answers, then weigh the pros and cons.

Pressure has advantages. Pressure defenses produce turnovers, thus increasing possession and sometimes easy baskets. They can demoralize and wear down an opponent. They can foil an offensive plan by forcing the other team to play a different style of game and undermine mismatches that normally are a problem for your team. They also can fuel a comeback.

Pressure has disadvantages. Most prominently, pressure is major risk-taking. Fouls can add up. Missed steals and rotations can, in a flash, create unfavorable numbers and open the door to easy transition baskets. An effective press is the product of extensive practice work, which may take away from other activities. If you want to have pressure defenses, you have to be all-in.

Ball Screen Defense

Screens are a way of life in basketball. Your players should learn a variety of ways to handle: (a) switching screens, (b) trapping off the ball screen, (c) showing (hedging) and recovering, (d) going under the screen (against non-shooting threats), and (e) fighting over the screen (for perimeter shooters). In addition, consider variations for certain game situations to surprise the opponent, like switching only bigs or only guards.

Don't take screen defense technique lightly. Like so many other skills, repetition will help your athletes execute well. Flaws in screen defense can lead to consistently bad results. Also, use code names for how you want them to handle screens in game situations.

Specialty Defensive Teams

Consider specialty teams on defense for specific game situations, comprised in whole or in part, of your best: (a) on-the-ball defenders, (b) defensive rebounders, (c) rim protectors, (d) perimeter defenders, and (e) matchup zone defenders. Again, depending on the situation, consider a combination of these skill sets, each calculated to get a stop and limit the other team to a single opportunity on a possession.

Brief Thoughts
on Offense

Crafting an offense transforms a coach into the
sports equivalent of an artist creating on canvass.
The marketplace is flooded with Xs and Os ideas,
and you have wide berth to give expression to your philosophy and imagination to establish a menu for success at the offensive end of the floor, including inspired
original creations. Also, don't be so quick to throw out
the entire system of your predecessor. There is value in
continuity. See what your predecessor featured that is
well-suited for your team.

Systems

There are essentially two schools of thought on selecting an offensive system, either you: (1) believe so

strongly in a particular way to play (e.g., a dribble-drive motion offense) that you rely on it each year regardless of personnel (the Program System) or (2) favor mixing up offenses each year to adapt, as necessary, to changing personnel (the Adjustable System). While both styles can co-exist, they each have distinct advantages and disadvantages.

The Program System. One important advantage of running the same offense each year—especially if you have the lower level teams do likewise—is substantially limiting the time you must spend teaching the system year after year. Even if the other program teams, like the junior varsity, don't follow suit, the incremental teaching burden is confined to new varsity players. The related benefit is that players generally have a longer stretch of time to refine execution of the system. The main, and obvious, disadvantage is that personnel may not always be well suited for what you want to do, which, during the course of a season, can cause frustration, impair commitment, and lower the odds of success. It can also, in the long term, undermine the program goal of seamless continuity. And, more immediately, you can be scouted more easily.

The Adjustable System. The main advantage of this system is that it is tailored closely to the skills and talents of the specific players each year. The residual advantage is that it makes scouting your team more difficult every year. The disadvantages are the flip side of the Program System: more time teaching and less transferable value extracted from prior work.

Which school of thought you embrace or where you fall on the continuum between the two schools, will depend on a blend of coaching philosophy and personal style. So long as you are comfortable that where you wind up is calculated to place your players in the best situations to succeed, you are in good shape.

The Offense Smorgasbord

There are seemingly endless offensive sets from which to choose and tinker with, depending on what you conclude will work best for your team. Here is a broad (and simplified) sampling.

Transition. Little need be said about the attributes of an offense built around the transition game. The keys to success are conditioned athletes, well-identified roles, spacing, precision in attack, and smart decisions with the ball.

Read and React. This system is built on developed habits and is adaptable to most any player. As a result, it has the potential for being used year to year even if faced with major player turnover. It places core responsibility in a central ballhandler as others read the defense and react to make plays.

Princeton. A deliberate, slower approach that requires discipline and basketball IQ, this offense emphasizes motion, screens on and off the ball, crisp passing, and, famously, the back door cut. It is not what comes to mind for coaches who cherish uptempo or rely chiefly on perimeter shooting.

Pick and Roll. The pick and roll (and its cousin the pick and pop) continues in vogue. It is especially effective if the two players working off each other are fungible talents, which makes double teaming the ballhandler off the screen risky. When they are not fungible, ball screens can create mismatches and, for teams that space well, good looks for three-point shooters. Good decisions with the ball off screens are essential.

Motion. A system that relies heavily on patience, passing, and five players moving, its effectiveness turns on players being comfortable in each position. The beauty of this offense, apart from its visual artistry, is that it is difficult to scout, mostly because when executed well, players make basketball decisions on the fly based on how the defense responds.

Continuity. Similar in appearance to the motion offense, the continuity offense relies on players filling specific roles to create a pattern that repeats until an opportunity arises. It is a deliberate and slow offense that can wear a defense down, leading to defensive lapses that generate high percentage shots. It can also be predictable and, thus, easy to scout.

Triangle. The triangle (aka the triple-post) offense utilizes spacing, interchangeable players, ball reversal, automatic passes from set spots, constant off-the-ball player movement, penetration, and the ability to read defenses. In all its splendor and dimension, it is too complex for most high schools, but contains parts that can be extracted effectively as a supplemental offense (e.g., using a simplified form of the sideline triangle's basket cuts and weakside options to create high percentage shots).

Set Offenses (Specific Plays). No matter what offense you use, the playbook should include several set plays—highly structured sets with beginnings and endings. The endings should allow players easily to shift into your main system or another play whenever nothing materializes from the particular play. In addition, include quick hitters in the playbook, which are best in discrete, time-sensitive situations like the end of quarters.

Zone. No matter how you feel about zone defense, you *will* see it and must prepare for it. In a nutshell, the objectives of zone offense are moving defenders with passing (including ball reversal) and pass fakes, attacking and exploiting gaps in the zone, either with dribble penetration or flashing players, and getting the ball inside the interior of the defense (which can open up various scoring opportunities). You can also use screens, especially back screens, to free up shooters and create penetration lanes. Consider having at least two zone offenses.

Press Offense. Add a press breaker from the start and practice it often. Make the press more difficult in practice than what the team can expect in games, like pitting seven defenders against five offensive players, limiting the offense to passes only, or combinations and variations of both.

Baseline Out of Bounds (BLOB). Have several BLOB plays in your playbook, including against man and zone defenses and for different specific situations (e.g., several seconds left on the shot clock or in the quarter).

Sideline Out of Bounds (SLOB). One or two SLOB plays are nice playbook additions, especially for specific situations where you need or want a quick score or expect the other team to challenge (and deny) the inbounds pass.

Breakdown Drills

While selection of an offensive system is an essential first step, the next is more important: working toward precise execution through habit building. Distill the offense into separate parts so the team can practice each piece regularly, preferably in two groups (each in the half court to minimize time). Breakdown drills will help ensure that the movements, cuts, communication, and spacing are second nature and instinctive, a form of muscle memory.

Improving the Offense

As the season advances, look for aspects of the offense that need tweaking. Don't stubbornly cling to your selection or creation if it is not doing what it is designed to do. Keep your eye on what is necessary for the team to succeed.

Consider, too, adding plays or systems in anticipation of league competition or after league gets underway to offset opposition scouting of what you showed during preseason (or early league play). This includes BLOB and SLOB plays (as well as what you do on defense). Don't overload the team; be narrow and focused. But diversifying your arsenal can give your team a new edge.

Offensive Skills

The list of "little things" and individual skills on the offensive side of the ledger is seemingly endless and what you emphasize is your call. Here is a list to use.

1. *Ballhandling and Dribbling.* The ability to be facile with the ball is the foundation for many skills, including dribbling, passing, receiving, shooting, and rebounding. Make ballhandling drills a mainstay of practices.

2. *Passing.* There are five passes to master: chest, skip, bounce, outlet, and baseball. Teach passers to know their receivers. Not every player can catch the ball with the same skill or in the same way.

Also, ask yourself this: are behind-the back and one-handed passes permissible in your program?

3. *Catching the Basketball.* Receiving the ball and getting ready to execute off the catch is as basic a skill as any. Players have to learn to catch securely—without eagerly anticipating the next moment.

4. *The Loose Ball.* Going after loose balls is an often-ignored skill. Teach players how to dive for the ball and recover. Forbid them from trying to control a loose ball with the dribble. It is better to secure the ball and slow things down for a moment than move with too much urgency and jeopardize the possession. John Wooden: "Be quick, but don't hurry."

5. *The Triple-Threat Position.* This is a fundamental skill that often gets ignored. You can combine it with other activities, including shooting and dribble drive drills, as well as when working on your half court offense.

6. *The Upfake.* One of the most effective moves in basketball, it gets executed too little in games. Include the upfake in as many drills as practical. It should be ingrained.

7. *The Jump Stop.* Arguably, the jump stop is the single most valuable offensive move, but often gets little player respect. The well-executed jump shot can give a team added momentum or even be a

game changer. It strengthens interior penetration, tends to freeze the defense, allows multiple
scoring opportunities, minimizes turnovers and
bad shots, and generates foul calls. Preach the
jump stop!

8. *The Pass Fake.* Especially against pressure and
   zone defenses, this is another "little thing" honored more in the breach. It creates opportunities
   and minimizes turnovers.

9. *The Jab Step.* Most players have a jab step, but they
   need more work combining the move with other
   skills, like the up and pass fakes and the rip-thru
   (next).

10. *Rip-thru.* Often practiced in conjunction with the
    upfake and jab step, the rip-thru, followed by an
    aggressive penetration step on the outside of the
    defender, can ignite an attack on the defense.

11. *Cutting to the Basket.* Your offensive sets and break-
    down drills will identify specific cuts on which
    your players should focus.

12. *Attacking the Basket.* The ability of a team to attack
    the basket is directly proportionate to their abil-
    ity to be game-competitive. Dribble penetration
    opens up *team* opportunities, especially when
    combined with the *jump stop.*

13. *Finishing Through Contact.* Similarly, the ability to
    attack the basket and play through contact is
    essential. Players often shy away or anticipate

contact and alter their finishes, with less than desirable results. Use karate-style kicking pads to bang players during layup drills to help them learn to finish strong.

14. *Post Moves.* There are an assortment of post moves to teach post players, including the drop-step, up-and-under, up fake, interior crab dribble, reverse and inside pivots, and the jump hook, as well as how to gain advantageous post position, and catch the ball safely in the post and re-post. Especially if you use stations, work closely with low post players on a collection of techniques and skills.

15. *Shooting.* Work on shots in practice that your players are expected to get in games, which is not always what players like to do! Practice drills at game speed and intensity. For example, passing is an important part of any shooting drill. A sloppy pass often means a sloppy shot.

16. *Free Throws.* Free throws are often the difference between a win and a loss. Track performance each day. Make them a priority in practice.

17. *The "Weak" Hand.* Require use of the weak hand for advantage, especially on finishes at the basket and dribbling.

18. *Rebounding.* Close games turn on a few possessions. Offensive rebounds give you extra possessions. Therefore...

19. *Screens.* There is much to do in the realm of screens offensively: how to set, use, slip, reject, and roll off them. Two-on-two and three-on-three drills provide an effective practice structure to develop these skills.

20. *Jumping.* You can enhance hops with early-season conditioning drills.

21. *Speed.* Select drills that emphasize speed, including short bursts and stop and go.

As is evident, an offense contains a wide range of component parts. The conundrum is that it's not realistic to focus on all of them equally—that would give short shrift to other important parts of your practices. Skill work during the offseason, especially the summer (see Chapter 21), can ease the pressure of practice time allocation during the season. Emphasize what you value and seek a balance, knowing that the teaching process has many beginnings but no ends.

Games

ame management is where the rubber meets the coaching road. It is a distinct skill with its own learning curve, requiring substantial time and experience to hone. Being a great practice coach does not make you a great game coach and vice versa. You might be able to teach a variety of skills your first day as a head coach, but being a game coach does not so easily follow.

When it comes to managing games, an interesting dichotomy exists between *coaching* and *managing*. On the one hand, when we don our manager hat, we make decisions and direct players in an effort to impact game outcome. Our contributions as managers in game situations are specific, direct, and plain. On the other hand, wearing our coaching shirt, we facilitate experiences to help players enjoy long-term improvement and pursue goals. As such, our influence can be subtle and might not manifest for months or years. Both roles co-exist during games (e.g., whether to make an immediate impact on the game or influence long-term player development regardless of game impact) and coaches must be astute enough to discern the differences and know when one takes precedence over the other.

That said, there is much for coaches to know and do when it comes to game competition.

Rules

The National Federation of State High School Associations (NFHS) is the umbrella organization for sports and other high school activities. Its mission statement is:

> The National Federation of State High School Associations serves its members, related professional organizations and students by providing leadership for the administration of education-based interscholastic activities, which support academic achievement, good citizenship and equitable opportunity.

As a membership organization, the NFHS, among other things, sponsors conferences and sports programs, oversees a learning center, maintains a blog (*We Are High School*), publishes materials on sports and education, has its own Hall of Fame, maintains statistics, issues awards, and, more to the current topic, issues game rules for each high school sport. While local high school organizations are free to modify rules to fit their circumstances, by and large the NFHS rules govern, including for basketball.

It is not expected that as the head coach you be conversant with the full array of NFHS basketball rules, but you may want to be familiar with the rules that cover recurring game situations, as well as the rules your league has adopted specifically to supplement NFHS requirements. In addition, consider having a copy of the NFHS basketball rulebook accessible during the season, especially at games. You'll never know when it will come in handy. The rules are also available electronically (via Amazon). Your league or sports section should inform you each year of rule changes. NFHS posts them timely on its website as well. It is not a bad idea to become an NFHS member to stay current on relevant developments and have access to its many resources.

Scrimmages

Coaches generally are free to organize scrimmages however they please. For example, you can keep score on a quarter-by-quarter basis, resetting the scoreboard at 0-0 each quarter. You can use five 10-minute running quarters or regular game rules. Clear any structural changes with the officials, who usually will cooperate, although they might push back if proposed changes increase their time commitment too much. They generally get paid by the event, not the hour.

You also can agree on playing zone or use full court pressure for one or two periods so each team has an opportunity to run zone offense and handle the press. Experiment also with different lineups and substitution patterns to learn more about your talent. The bottom line is that "winning" the scrimmage, which the players always want to do, and which part of you will also want to do, is less important than getting long term value out of the experience.

Scouting Opponents

You will want as much advance information about opponents as is reasonably obtainable. You have several options: (a) scout games personally with or without staff, (b) film games involving upcoming opponents or get film from other coaches, (c) debrief other coaches who have good information on an opponent, (d) consult sites like MaxPreps that have detailed statistical information on teams, or (e) combinations of the above.

It is important to sit down with your staff early in the season to prepare a scouting schedule that harmonizes with your practice and game schedule, and contains a comprehensive plan for scouting as many opponents as possible. Scouting is time consuming and will require some travel. You might need to call on others outside your staff to help.

Some important things to gain from a scout of an upcoming opponent are:
1. Your initial defensive matchups.
2. Strengths and weaknesses.
3. Rebounding ability.
4. Poor foul shooters.
5. Excellent foul shooters.
6. Ball handlers who can be pressured.
7. Three-point shooters to watch.
8. How best to defend against their half court offense and BLOB and SLOB plays.
9. What will work offensively against them.
10. Anything the other team does that requires special preparation such as press, traps, an uncommon zone (like a 1-3-1), transition game techniques, heavy reliance on the low post, and so on.

Prepare a written scouting report for your players to review sufficiently in advance of the game. The report should be detailed, but not too long (typically two pages), and should cover the various items discussed above. Include a short bullet point list of Keys to Victory. In addition, where practical, hold a film session to review the opponent in a prior game.

Game Checklist

Statistical Sheets. As discussed in Chapter 8, find a game-knowledgeable person(s) to keep stats. Create a sheet to use each game. You can log shots taken and makes (2s and 3s), steals, assists, turnovers, blocks, charges drawn, deflections, individual and team rebounds (offensive and defensive), by quarter, the half and the entire game.

Medical Kit. Make sure medical kits are always well stocked, especially with ice packs, Band-Aids, and gauze. An assistant (or team manager) should be responsible for bringing the medical kit to the bench and retrieving it after the game.

Scorebook. See the Chapter 8 discussion about identifying volunteers to handle scorebook responsibilities. Your away game scorebook keeper should coordinate during the game with the home team scorebook person, who maintains the "official" book, to make sure the books continue to match. This is especially important for tracking fouls and time-outs.

Team Rosters. Bring printouts of your roster to games for the other team to use. It is a well-appreciated courtesy. You can also tape a copy to the inside of your scorebook. Most roster sheets include player name, uniform number, and school year. Some add position, height, and weight. For scorebook purposes, you only need names and numbers. Be mindful of the scorebook rules, including that teams must fill out their roster and identify starters by a certain time, commonly 10 minutes before tipoff. Violation of the rule can earn you a pre-opening tip team technical.

Have someone double-check the official book to make sure all eligible players are listed with the correct uniform number, including latecomers, as well as slightly injured or ill players who are suited up and might be used in a pinch. If they are not in the book, they cannot play. Note, too, that while most referees tend to overlook late roster entries, incorrect uniform numbers normally draw a technical. Finally, check the other team's scorebook as soon as it ready to confirm starters and reaffirm matchup assignments. Surprises can happen to impact pregame defensive assignments.

Game Balls. Have four to six game balls for away games, which an assistant (or team manager) should bring, distribute during warm-ups and retrieve after pregame and halftime warmups. Balls get lost easily. Make sure someone is on top of this.

Game Day Protocol. Consider a game day ritual for your players to generate a collective vibe on campus. You can have the team eat lunch together on game day. While getting 100 percent attendance may not always practical, it is an excellent team-building habit. You can also require players to dress a certain way on game day. Both routines convey a sense of pride and togetherness.

Coaching Dress Attire. Unless your school has a dress code for its coaches, which is not usual, you have discretion to dress as you see fit for games. As can easily be seen, the coaching culture includes a wide range of game attire. Whatever you choose, keep this in mind:

you are an ambassador for the school and a role model for your players. In addition, if your players are expected to dress a certain way on game day, set an example and dress accordingly.

Pregame Team Meeting

You should consider carefully what to say to your team before a game. Put your comments on paper. Don't wing it. Summarize your points on the white board in the locker room for the pregame meeting. Do not allow distractions during the pregame. All eyes should be on you and everyone in sharp listening mode.

Identify specific game goals (e.g., more than 30 team rebounds or fewer than 5 turnovers per half). Stress the keys to victory for the game such as stopping a particular shooter or slowing down the transition game, or, for your team, controlling the glass, getting to the rim often, or establishing an inside game.

Be dialed-in but calm. Get them focused and moderately inspired, but not too emotionally pumped. They have a job to do that requires clarity of mind and purpose. Reinforce their strengths. Give them something specific on which to focus to start the game (e.g., "everyone touches the ball before we attack the basket in our first possession"). Remind them of what they control, and, if they execute the game plan, they will emerge victorious.

If your pre-game talks go about 10-15 minutes, assemble the team in the locker-room about 25-30 minutes before game time. Generally, you want 15 minutes for warm-ups. An assistant should monitor the time during the pre-game meeting. You can save a final thought for the huddle before the starting five takes the floor.

Set a family tone in the locker room. Have everyone hold hands or put arms around in a circle for the final chant. Constantly stress family principles.

Game Management

Substitutions. Apart from an established starting five, it is a challenge to know who to play, with what teammates, and in what situations. And, of course, there is the ever-constant concern about opportunities to contribute or OTC (aka playing time or PT). Some coaches like to play the entire squad in the first half and substitute in the second half strategically to win. Each coach has to manage each game as they see fit in the circumstances. Discuss substitution issues with assistants before the game (e.g., "we need to play Jody more in the first half") and have an assistant remind you of this during the game. Make sure your players know the substitution rules and procedures. Here is a reminder list.

1. Players should enter the game with a tucked-in jersey.

2. Substitutes should move to the designated spot in front of the scorer's table.

3. Substitutes should report specifically to the official scorer.

4. Substitutes should wait until the referee waves them in before coming on the floor.

5. Replaced players should run off the floor and interact with the substitute about the defensive assignment.

6. The entire bench should greet players coming off the floor.

7. When a substitution during foul shots is designed to stop the action after a make on the last foul shot, the substitution should *not* report to the scorer's table until after the referee *delivers the ball* to the foul shooter on the *final* foul shot; reporting beforehand brings the sub into the game before the foul shot and foils the stoppage strategy.

8. In contrast, a substitution for a player in foul trouble should seek entry to the game on the first foul shot; this way, you avoid keeping the substituted player in the game if the last foul shot is missed.

Dealing with Substituted Players. While not easy, it is good practice to talk briefly with players when they come off the floor, especially if they are not playing well or you perceive that being taken out will unsettle them. If you cannot speak with them right away because of the game situation, which often happens, enlist an assistant for this purpose. If that is not practical, get to them later when time permits. Don't forget them.

Time-outs. Every coach has a different approach to time-outs. You might use them sparingly, preferring your athletes to figure things out for themselves and in the process reap long-term benefits. You might use them less in early preseason for the same reason. You might have a more structured approach, preferring to save a minimum number of time-outs for the end of the game. You might tend to be game-specific, playing each game by ear. And, you might like to use shorter time-outs first and longer ones later in the game.

Keep in mind that regardless of your approach, high school players, especially younger players, need a break in the action sometimes to refocus and get reminders, especially during stressful and pressure-packed patches of games like crunch time of a close game.

Importantly, use lulls in the action to accomplish the same things as a formal time-out without calling one. Those "free" timeouts include the following:

1. When a player fouls out you can confer with the remaining four on the floor (20 seconds);
2. Game delays (e.g., player injury or clock malfunction) allow a coach to assemble the team for a meeting (indeterminate amount of time)
3. Quarter break (60 seconds);
4. Anticipating the other team's time-out can save you one (30 or 60 seconds)

5. Three foul shots allow you to bring the team to-
    gether during the first two (10-20 seconds)
6. The first foul shot of two allows you to confer
    with your point guard or others (5-10 seconds)
7. Substitutions can convey information to the team
    on floor to save a time-out
8. Dead balls (e.g., ball out of bounds, substitutions,
    and foul shots) allow a quick team assembly on
    the floor without the coach

Why you call time-outs is another art. Time-outs are
called to:
1. Break the other team's momentum.
2. Change game strategy.
3. Relax and motivate your team.
4. Design a specific play.
5. Ice a free throw shooter.
6. Instruct on specific plays or address defenses not
    being executed properly.
7. Give your players a rest.
8. Prepare for the final minutes of a close game.
9. Prepare for a final possession.
10. Substitute players.
11. Get a player in foul trouble off the floor.

Time-out Routines. Have a routine for players to follow for
time-outs. For example, have your players on the floor
sprint to the bench when a time-out is called. A quick
assembly preserves precious time-out seconds and

maintains good team energy and camaraderie. Further, during a full time-out some coaches insist players stay on the floor and others have the game players sit on chairs and face the coach while the rest of the team huddles around. Some schools use a huddle format with everyone standing with their arms around each other. There are variations. Regardless of your preferences, be consistent.

Fouls. You need to know who to foul when behind and to stop the clock. You or an assistant should know the poorest foul shooters on the floor. Similarly, be on top of *when* you have opportunities to use a foul-to-give strategy, not only down the stretch, but also at the end of the first half.

Bench Rules. These can vary depending on your philosophy. Example rules to consider, including some game rules, are:

1. Bench players should greet teammates coming off the floor.
2. Bench players must never stand up during games, except to substitute, during time-outs and to greet players coming off the floor.
3. Assistants also should not stand, except for time=outs and greeting players coming off the floor.
4. Assistants should *never* speak to the referees.

5. Bench players should cheer positively and encourage teammates. They should *not* belt out coaching instructions.

6. Players who enter the game during a time-out should sit on the bench with the other four players for the full time-out.

Entering the Gym for Pregame Warm-ups. Teams generally like to determine how they will enter the gym to warm up. Whatever the routine, it should be organized, smooth. and classy.

Warm-up Drills. Players should get loose and break a slight sweat. You can pick the warm-up drills in consultation with the team or have the team pick them subject to your approval. The team should work on its warm-up drills in practice early in the season.

Halftime Protocol. Every coach has a protocol for halftime. Some meet first with the coaching staff to review what to stress in the locker room and, as they do, players do the same separately as a team. When coaches rejoin the team, they hear what the players have to say—through one representative—and provide their own comments. Be positive at halftime, no matter what the situation. While sometimes you may need to resort to tough talk, do so selectively, otherwise it becomes old fast and falls on deaf ears.

Be mindful, too, of taking too much time in the locker room, especially if you want your players to get some shots up before the second half starts. An assistant can monitor the time.

Postgame Protocol. Here, too, coaches differ. Stress what the team did well (thus specific to the game), take stock on where the team is at that part of the season (the current big picture), and identify areas for improvement (looking to the future). Allow your assistants and players to comment at some point.

On what hopefully is a rare occasion, when the team really needs to soul search, you may want to hear from every player after a game. Not every player will step up voluntarily in that situation, prompting the need to "call on them" like in a traditional classroom. They always have something to say, however, once they get started.

The Care and Feeding of Referees

How coaches relate to referees in games is an underappreciated and underutilized leadership opportunity. Every game contains multiple referee situations—ready-made role model moments—where coaches can demonstrate effective communication, consistency between what they preach and what they do, tolerance of mistakes (which we all make), self-control (of frustration), and basic human respect. Sometimes it is easier said than done, especially in the heat of a scalding hot moment. But there is no denying that these valuable leadership moments routinely arise and no denying that we coaches sometimes miss the boat on them. We owe it to our players, officials, and ourselves, the values of the program we steward, and, not the least, the integrity of the game we love, to pay keen attention to this part of what we do. Games come and go, but the lessons we teach and the behavior we model endure.

The Referee World

As with most aspects of life, when it comes to relationships, it helps to see the world through the eyes of others, an exercise that broadens and balances our perspective and refines how we see things. Here are observations from the referee vantage point:

1. Referees do what they do because they love the game—like we do. Indeed, many are former coaches and players.

2. The referee's primary responsibility is to facilitate a safe and fair game in accordance with the rules. They don't care who wins. The perfect game, from the standpoint of a referee, is a fair contest with no whistles.

3. Referees are not enemies, but rather an integral part of how the game is played.

4. Referees expect good sportsmanship.

5. Referees do not merely show up for games. They devote substantial time going through on-court and classroom training, studying the rules, breaking down games on film afterwards, and discussing game situations among themselves to improve their performance. They want to get it right.

6. Referees appreciate small doses of respect. A simple "hello, how are you doing" before the game, reinforced by an occasional "please" and "thank you" during the game, go a long way.

7. Referees operate from a clean slate each game. What is past is past.

8. Referees are well trained, but how well they conduct themselves might not always be apparent. For example, they might not go after a ball that rolls out of bounds, not because they don't want to bother, but because they are trained to keep their eyes on the court.

9. Referees expect head coaches to manage their benches, including assistants. By rule, only the head coach is permitted to speak with referees and stand during game action. Too many benches are undisciplined.

10. Referees appreciate help from coaches dealing with out-of-control people in the stands. They don't want to throw mom out of the gym.

11. New and less experienced referees may use the rule book more often than seasoned referees as they develop a feel for the game—like new coaches have to do!

12. Contrary to popular belief, referees do not like to issue technicals to coaches. They don't want to take the game out of players' hands because of coach behavior.

The Coach World: Game Standards

The flip side is what coaches can do to improve the quality of the experience for everyone.

Game Etiquette

1. When your team is the game host, make the officials feel comfortable and welcome on arrival and get them what they need to be game-ready.
2. Have the table personnel, clock, and scorebook ready to go 10 minutes prior to game time. It makes their job a little easier.
3. At the conclusion of each game, try to make eye contact with the officiating crew and thank them, no matter how you believe they did. They work hard for the betterment of the game.
4. Similarly, have your players thank the referees for officiating after the game. It is a good habit for them to develop.
5. Some referees are fine being addressed by their first names, but some are not. If you prefer being on a first-name basis with a referee—an informality that can improve communication—make sure the referee is fine interacting on that basis.

Referee Interaction

1. Chat with the referees before the game if you want to call attention to an issue likely to arise in the game (e.g., an opposing player with a tendency to

violate a particular rule). If you do, don't be surprised if the referees elect to have the other coach join the discussion to eliminate any appearance of favoritism.

2. Referees assume only the head coach will call time-outs. If you want your assistants also to be recognized for this purpose, inform the officials before the game.

3. Stress effective communication to your players. The more they carp, the less support they will get, and the more likely referees will resolve doubt against them. This includes non-verbal whining, like the infamous eye roll or the disdainful smirk.

4. Referees have feelings like the rest of us and want to perform well. If you do not like how referees are calling the game, getting in their faces won't improve things. If anything, it will make things worse. How do you like people to speak to you?

5. Similarly, you can expect a referee to explain a call, but not the underlying rule. Discussing rules takes time away from game focus. If necessary, discuss the rule after the game or another time.

6. Voice your views in the form of a question. For example: "Can you please tell me where the contact was on that foul?" In contrast, don't bark your curiosity this way: "No way that was a foul!" The former is more effective for getting your views heard.

7. If you adamantly disagree with a foul call on one of your players, don't give solace to the player by saying within earshot of the official, "the ref missed it."

8. Pick your spots with referees carefully. Too much complaining creates a boy-crying-wolf syndrome, and when you have a justified complaint, it could fall on deaf ears.

9. If an official beckons you to attend to an injured player, don't use the time to engage the officials about whether they could have prevented the injury in some way or other commentary about how the game is being officiated.

10. Consider occasionally complimenting a referee for a good call. They might not acknowledge the gesture, but they will appreciate it.

11. Referees, players, and coaches each make mistakes. It is part of the process. You don't want another adult in your face about coaching mistakes you make, right?

12. If an official says, "I might have missed it, coach," say thank you and let it go. No more need be said.

13. Sometimes, it is better to stay mum for long stretches of time, like the entire first half, and later quietly approach the referees, either directly or through a captain ("our coach wants me") to address something of concern (e.g., "No. 10 keeps grabbing our player's jerseys. Can you please

keep an eye out for that?"). Seek effective ways to achieve your goals.

14. There is little point complaining when a referee is in the right position to make a judgment call. The ref will not change their mind and, in that situation, there will not likely be a make-up call coming your way later.

Game Management

1. From time to time, remind your players that their job is to play, yours to coach, and the referees' to officiate. Underscore they should focus only on what they can control, and they cannot control the referees.

2. Remind them too that a referee never "wins" or "loses" a game. No matter how close the game, wins and losses result from the totality of all play, starting with the jump ball.

3. Never let a referee affect your ability to coach or your team's ability to play.

4. Similarly, if you spend a ton of time complaining to the officials, you model negativity for your players. Quickly and politely let your opinion be heard and then resume coaching. The more you complain, the less you are coaching.

5. If one of your players gets a technical foul, whether you think it is warranted or not, immediately substitute for that player, even for one possession.

The substitution sends a message to the officials you are handling it and (hopefully) offers a teaching moment to the player.

6. Similarly, if an official asks for help dealing with an on-court player, politely ask what occurred, immediately substitute for the player, and address the official's concerns.

7. Unless in a jurisdiction with the "seatbelt rule," which glues coaches to the bench except for specific situations (e.g., to call a time-out, approach the scorer's table, talk to an official, or cheer a play), be mindful of coaching box parameters. While officials are often lax in enforcing the coaching box limits if you are teaching, if you're complaining while outside the box so that you are a distraction, you risk getting a warning or an immediate technical. If you get a warning only, but the behavior continues, you likely will be issued a technical.

8. If the officials are not handling an opposing belligerent coach, at an appropriate dead ball, calmly (and even tongue-in-cheek) ask an official if you may act the same way without repercussion. That might inspire them to handle the other coach.

9. If officials are calling the game a certain way, like letting contact go generally, or, conversely, calling a tight physical game, tell the team to adjust to the tendency rather than get frustrated.

10. Do not tolerate fans heckling referees. When it happens, do what you can to stop it or address it later in an appropriate forum.

11. On the other hand, if at game conclusion, you believe the officiating crew did an egregious job, do not confront them at that time. Unless you believe it was serious enough to require immediate attention (e.g., inappropriate behavior), wait at least twenty-four hours to let things calm down before taking action. If the cooling-off period does not dampen your ire, reduce your concerns to writing, sticking to facts and avoiding personal comments, and submit a report to the appropriate administrative personnel. If possible, include filmed portions of what occurred.

Educational Measures

In addition to modeling good behavior in games, you can take additional steps to improve interactions with referees and advance program goals.

First, invite a referee to a practice to demonstrate application of certain rules for players, like traveling, blocks vs. charges, "carrying" the ball and hand-checking, or to discuss game etiquette and other relevant subjects.

Second, have your AD arrange an interactive forum for referees and league coaches to discuss various game rules and issues. Communication can be a great teacher and salve for what is otherwise contentious.

Third, have players alternate as officials for some intra-squad scrimmages. They will learn the rules better, experience first-hand the fruitless challenge of calling a flawless game, and get a sense of what it is like to endure player complaints. To facilitate, you or an assistant can play-act the role of the harsh bench coach. They might learn the value of tolerating mistakes.

Seek to build an environment of mutual respect with officials. Your players will benefit immeasurably, and you will improve the quality of games and give powerful expression to program values.

The Postseason Party

The postseason gathering is the season's grand finale, a time to put the entire journey into perspective, be grateful for the ride, appreciate (with the benefit of distance) the season highs and lows, and pay tribute to everyone who, each in their way, contributed to the communal experience. It is a time for a unique form of closure, as the season represents the only time the current composition of youth and adults will participate in this type of experience together. Each season is special for that reason alone, a once-in-a-lifetime happening for a particular group. Honor everyone and treat the meeting with the respect it deserves.

As with the kickoff potluck, team parents should organize the final potluck and, with your help if necessary, the venue. Hold the party sooner rather than later.

Delay tends to rob the atmosphere of emotional thunder and connectivity.

As the leader of this ensemble, be prepared for a command performance in whatever way you think appropriate to put a crown on the seasonal expedition. Here are items to consider for your final presentation to the assembled multitudes.

1. You will have many people to thank and acknowledge. They typically will include:
   - The party hosts.
   - The team parents. Here, consider a gift like flowers or other modest offering.
   - Other volunteers: the scorebook, statistics, transportation, drivers, chaperones, team dinner hosts, game film, and snack bar.
   - Everyone who ever attended a game (a *group* thank you).
   - Team manager.
   - Cheerleaders (where applicable).
   - Trainer (where applicable).
   - Your assistant coaches.
   - If you are married or have a partner, them too!

2. Give a season overview. Briefly discuss the intangibles the players displayed and underscore any traditional measures of success that apply.

3. Consider mentioning specific season highlights (e.g., that incredible fourth quarter comeback and overtime win during league play).

4. Cite all noteworthy team and individual team statistical accomplishments (e.g., Joe led the league in assists and the team led the league in rebounds).

5. Announce season awards. The process for determining year-end awards presumably will mirror captain selection. Each school has its award categories (e.g., most valuable this or that and sometimes inspirational recognition like the "Coach's Award"). If the customary school awards do not fit your season for any reason, discuss it with the AD. Most will allow a customized award. For example, you might think the team does not have a single MVP and instead prefer a Most Valuable Offensive Player and Most Valuable Defensive Player. Be creative in how to honor those deserving.

6. Schools sometimes provide certificates and pins separately for returning varsity and new varsity players. If so, it is a good opportunity to say something brief and special about each player.

7. A word of caution: During the course of this event, you may mention the names of some players, but not necessarily each player. If distribution of available awards and other parts of your presentation do not recognize every player, consider finding a way to do so. If you recognize fewer than 100 percent of your players, you will hurt feelings (and hear about it).

8. Consider some special words for graduating seniors. They are about to embark on a special and exciting post-high school journey. For example:
   - Thank them for all they did for the program.
   - Encourage them to be true to themselves in their future endeavors.
   - Remind them there are no short cuts to success no matter what they do.
   - Encourage them to maintain a tireless work ethic and never take anything for granted.
   - Remind them of the value of preparation and attention to detail.
   - Urge them to never waver from a commitment to excellence.
   - Offer any other words of wisdom you feel moved to impart.
9. Finally, you might use this opportunity to let returning families know about your preliminary plans for the postseason, especially the summer basketball program. See Chapter 21.

The Offseason

The work of a committed high school basketball coach is rarely done. After taking the requisite deep breaths once the season ends, you have to refocus and plan the spring and summer (and then the fall). (We covered planning the game, scrimmage, and practice schedule earlier.) Players committed to long-term improvement enjoy the greatest strides in the offseason, a goal substantially aided by a comprehensive postseason program. The additional benefit is the opportunity for the next round of teammates to work together over an extended period. Team cohesion and chemistry are powerful attributes that take time to nurture and develop.

The Spring and the Fall

Open Gym Activities. As always, know what the rules allow during the school year after (and before) the basketball season. Some jurisdictions forbid coaching during these sport hiatus periods and allow only "open gyms" where coaches are limited to supervising (like a chaperone), with no instruction permitted of any kind. This does not mean you cannot create a productive learning environment, only that you need to creatively devise an effective, fun, and practical format within the rules.

For starters, note that open gym has its ups and downs. The upside is kids enjoy improved conditioning (to some extent), there is a continued buzz about basketball at the school, and the players are drawn away from less productive activities. On the downside, open gyms tend to distill to undisciplined track meets, which reinforce bad habits and stunt skill growth.

One alternative is having basketball program leadership (presumably next year's seniors) organize open gyms at least in part around skill-development activities. They can figure this out with relative ease.

Another is to organize a 3-on-3 or 5-on-5 league with playoffs and a championship game. That format can keep everyone focused on competing on a team basis as each team vies to win the league title. Three on three in the half court has the added advantages of getting players to work closely with each other, utilize screens and cuts, and employ effective spacing. It also forces them to face focused on-the-ball defense and confront a steady diet of defensive help responsibility.

Be mindful that some basketball players in your program are multi-sport athletes who might not be available during the spring or fall. Set your expectations accordingly.

Scheduling Open Gyms. If you intend to hold open gyms, regardless of the format, reserve gym time early. For the spring, this means *before* the end of the season and for the fall as soon as possible after school resumes. There will be competition for gym space. Sitting idle too long risks coming up empty handed. The same applies to summer gym time (see below).

AAU and Club Ball. In addition to open gym, an effective way to keep the group together is to form an AAU or club team comprised largely of presumed returning and varsity-hopeful players. Again, beware of rules that might impact this option. The negative is that many players may have existing and even longstanding commitments to AAU or club programs, and it might be difficult and even sometimes ill-advised to pry them away.

Weight Room. Depending on schedule options, consider organizing a weight room program during the offseason.

The Summer

Summer Program Planning. The summer is an essential part of your program and must be approached with the same diligence and foresight as scheduling season games, scrimmages, and practices. Here are steps and considerations:

1. Determine first the period of time you are permitted to hold summer activities. Most jurisdictions allow you to start after graduation and go shortly until the first fall sport begins.

2. Devise a group communication method (e.g., email group) so you can communicate efficiently with interested families and players about summer plans, including incoming freshmen families (see below).

3. Prepare a summer practice schedule by working with the AD (or whomever else controls summer gym space) to allocate gym time. While competition for the gym time should be less than during the spring and fall, the other basketball program will likely want gym space, as well as possibly others.

4. Think carefully about how to group "teams" during the summer. For example, will you include everyone in one group or have Summer Varsity, Summer JV, and Summer Freshmen teams or some other combination? Balance playing opportunities, team and skill development, coaching resources, and efficiency.

5. Think specifically about what to accomplish in practices. The summer is an ideal time for focused work on select skills and parts of your system, as

well as aspects of conditioning and weight work. Think ahead to the upcoming season and what stage of skill development, conditioning, and systems knowledge you would like to see when next season starts. Build the foundation you want for the upcoming season.

6. While working on the practice schedule, identify competitive activities, including scrimmages with other schools, summer leagues, and tournaments. Be aware of deadlines for applying for some activities, especially tournaments. Presumably, you will have information on prior summer activities available to consider.

7. If you host scrimmages, remember you need referees, which must be arranged sufficiently in advance and cost money (which you can split with the other schools).

Summer Program Costs. Quickly figure out the costs of the summer activities. Total costs may vary depending on the groups you set up. For example, you might have an incoming freshmen league, junior varsity tournament, and so on. You may need different cost schedules depending on how you organize summer player groups.

Set deadlines for collecting money from families to parse out who may or may not participate. Determine whether coaches may charge for their time. Some schools do not allow any charges other than a pass through of actual expenses associated with the activities.

Be sensitive to whether all families can afford the summer program. For those who cannot, identify options for supporting them. Do what you can not to turn away any family because of costs.

Incoming Freshmen. As soon as possible after the season ends, or earlier if practical, see if the school can provide a list of incoming freshmen interested in the basketball program, with contact information for them and their families. Making early contact will make summer planning more efficient, increase attendance, demonstrate program leadership, and highlight player and family inclusion. In addition, the school might allow you to include an informational insert in its new-admissions packet in the spring that briefly describes the summer program and invites direct contact with you.

Finally, consider holding an on-campus meeting before the summer for all incoming students interested in basketball and their families to introduce yourself, talk about your vision, expectations and program values, the summer program plan, scheduling for the next year, and answer questions.

Expectations for the Summer. Two expectation issues typically arise during the summer you might want to anticipate and address early.

First, what are your expectations about attendance during the summer? In some jurisdictions, rules do not permit mandatory attendance. Nonetheless, you want to extol the benefits of participation and reinforce, what everyone implicitly knows, that the value each player gains from the summer program is proportionate to the amount of time spent in the gym and weight room with teammates. At the same time, respectfully recognize that families have a variety of other plans during the summer and request that, at a minimum, families inform you early what planned activities, including practices, the player will attend.

Second, how does summer performance (and attendance) impact next year's tryouts, if at all? If summer attendance is not mandatory, the extent to which a player attends summer programs may not be used as a factor in team selection decisions. Be unambiguous that the coaching staff will *not* use summer performance as a criterion for tryouts.

Be clear, however, that the summer is not entirely irrelevant to tryouts. The more time a player devotes to skills and conditioning during the summer, the better chances of success at tryouts. Separation between players occurs during the summer. Players vying for a spot or role on any of the available teams should assess the relative importance of other summer activities against maximizing the ability to perform come tryouts. Urge athletes to conscientiously prioritize what is important to them: CDC (choices, decisions, and consequences).

The Care and Feeding of Yourself

The life of a high school varsity basketball head coach can be all-encompassing—emotionally, physically, and mentally. The time commitment alone is tiring. The pressure to succeed we impose on ourselves adds to the burden—and the expectations of others adds more weight. This is no complaint, mind you. It is to recognize that the job, packed with fun, inspiration, meaning, and much more, is demanding and draining.

It is important to decompress regularly and develop healthy habits that give your life balance. For example, instead of going home after a game and obsessing—as compelling as that might feel—spend time instead with loved ones, read a book, see a movie, or do something fulfilling unrelated to hoops to reboot your system and clear your head. Seek experiences that remove you from the action now and then. Create perspective through distance. Know what you are experiencing inside and be true to yourself.

Identify and seek out coach mentors, more experienced coaches who can be useful sounding boards and provide sound counsel. Don't do it alone. Talk to others whose judgment you respect and trust.

Be open to change and be honest with yourself. Sometimes old habits stymie success and, equally bad, are sources of frustration. Check in with yourself to see whether what worked in the past needs retooling or discarding. Embrace your mistakes as teaching moments. As you lead your teams on a journey each year, remember you are on your own never-ending ride of personal and professional growth.

Coaching is a special calling with untold benefits, not only for the athletes, school, and community, but for you personally as well. Constantly seek to make the right decisions for *you* in your life and do whatever is reasonably possible to stay in balance.

Conclusion

Coaching at the high school level is a special calling. It is a privilege, an honor, and a fascinating experience. It is an opportunity to share and teach something intrinsically meaningful and at the same time help youth develop tools to navigate life challenges and find contentment well beyond their high school days. Work hard to improve each day, grow personally and professionally, and be ever mindful that the learning path is infinite. Appreciate each moment and bask in the vast potential of the undertaking.

Acknowledgements

Thank you to my talented and loving son Coach **Aidan Coffino**, who inspired the writing of this book and later took the time to provide feedback on the draft manuscript. His insights and editorial comments were, not surprisingly, invaluable and his commitment to the youth he coaches is second to none.

Thank you to my other talented and loving son Coach **Torin Coffino**, who honored me beyond measure by asking me, after I retired from coaching, to be his assistant when he got his first high school head coaching gig. That privilege gifted me the chance to see him grow as a coach each day and gave me an enlightened coaching perspective from the vantage point of eighteen inches from the head coaching seat.

Thank you Coach **Chris Lavdiotis**, the talented head coach of the boys' varsity team of Lowell High School, for your friendship, support, and review and comments on the draft manuscript. More than anything, I love basking in the passion you have for the game and your tireless devotion to your student-athletes.

I take a deep and reverent bow to my first high school athletic director, the incomparable **Eliot Smith** of Lick-Wilmerding High School in San Francisco, who mentored me as a varsity head coach and graciously provided contributions to the book. Coach Smith is a perpetual source of inspiration.

I am indebted to four other athletic directors who generously and enthusiastically provided me thoughtful perspectives on the core relationship between a high school head basketball head coach and athletic director: **Brendan Blakeley** (Head Royce School), **Josh Frechette** (Marin Academy), **Steve Glass** (The Bay School), and **Val Cubales** (Balboa High School).

I am forever grateful to three classy and talented referees—**Nancy Clary**, **Bill Black**, and **Larry Moyer**—each of whom blessed me with their wisdom for this book and never stopped teaching me about how to honor and work effectively with game officials.

Thank you David Wogahn of AuthorImprints for your sage advice, help, and guidance in getting this book published.

And not least, I tip my hat to a special friend—Coach **Steve Compagno** (legendary coach of Redwood High School)—for his unbridled passion for the game, his selfless mentoring of high school athletes, and his special contributions to this book.

About the Author

Before becoming a full-time writer, blogger, and editor, Michael Coffino had two parallel careers: one in the courtroom and the other in the gymnasium. He was a litigation and trial attorney for thirty-six years, as well as a legal writing instructor, and concurrently devoted twenty-four years as a basketball coach, primarily at the high school level. Since retiring from both, he has written five books, including *Prepping for Success*.

He is author of *The Other Classroom: The Essential Importance of High School Athletics* and *Odds-On Basketball Coaching: Crafting High-Percentage Strategies for Game Situations*. He is also the coauthor of a memoir titled *Play It Forward: From Gymboree to the Yoga Mat and Beyond*, released in 2016, and another memoir titled *My Life: A Story of Resilience and Love*, set for release the summer of 2019.

Michael also ghostwrites books, blogs, and articles and freelance edits. He is writing his first work of fiction and working on memoirs for other clients.

Michael grew up in the Bronx, in its Mott Haven and Highbridge neighborhoods. He plays guitar, holds a black belt in karate, and lives in Marin County, California. Michael has two adult sons, both teachers and high school basketball coaches.

Made in United States
North Haven, CT
22 June 2022

20531392R00115